W9-BFZ-751

Giants in the Land

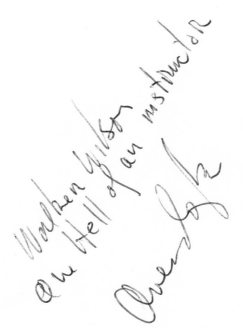

Giants in the Land

Folktales and Legends of Wisconsin

Dennis Boyer

with illustrations by Owen Coyle

PRAIRIE OAK PRESS
Madison, Wisconsin

First edition, first printing
Copyright © 1997 by Dennis Boyer

All rights reserved. No part of this publication may be reproduced or transmitted in any form or by any means, electronic or mechanical, including photocopy, recording, or any information storage or retrieval system, without permission in writing from the publisher.

Prairie Oak Press
821 Prospect Place
Madison, Wisconsin 53703

Typeset by Quick Quality Press, Madison, Wisconsin
Printed in the United States of America
by BookCrafters, Chelsea, Michigan

Library of Congress Cataloging-in-Publication Data

Boyer, Dennis.
   Giants in the land: folk tales and legends of Wisconsin / Dennis
Boyer; illustrated by Owen Coyle. -- 1st ed.
         p.   cm.
   ISBN 1–879483–45–9 (alk. paper)
   1. Tales—Wisconsin. 2. Legends—Wisconsin. I. Title.
GR110.W5B693 1997
398.2'09775—dc21   97-35598
                                                           CIP

For Donna, Lori, and Alexzandra
. . . my Wisconsin–Costa Rica
connections

Contents

Introduction . . . . *ix*

Part One
Heroes and Rogues—
Larger Than Life Characters

Badger Bill 3
Langlade's Wild Boy 7
Iron Lena and the Ladies from Hades 9
Rewey's "Scotch Giant" 13
Dirty Pierre 16
River Rat Fred 20
The Hiding Kickapoo 23
Wyalusing Snake Man 26
Picket Line Koski 30
Milwaukee's Juju Mama 33
Deer Camp Dick 36
Poker Run Pete 40
Trapper Tom 43
Walter the Warden 47
King of the Poachers 50
Fox River Coureur du Bois 54
Haystack Hilda 57
Washington's Last Soldier 60
Keeper of the Northern Lights 62
The Culdees of Doty Island 66
Plover's Waynabozo 69
Nels Niklaus of Scandinavia 73
The Welsh Prince 76

Ole Bolle 79
Apple Jack 83
Fritz Kleinnagel 87
Benton's Soldier Girl 90
Big Boris of Cornucopia. 93
Shawano's Geek. 95
Cranberry Charlie. 98

Part Two
Creature Feature—Wisconsin's Threatened and Threatening Species

Big Harry of Chequamegon 105
Coon Valley Trolls 108
Watertown's Elbedritzel 111
The Willy Wooly of Kidrick Swamp. 113
The Sprague Stumper-Jumper. 116
The Giant Brown Swiss 120
The Little Hodag 123
Porte des Morts Wiitiko 127
Trempealeau's Buffabob Herd 130
The Dwarf Mastodons of Boaz. 132
Lake Winnebago's Giant Sturgeon 135

Part Three
Lessons and Legacies— Teaching Through Stories

The Shining Boy. 141
Black River's Gloomnadoom 143
St. Croix River's Little People 145
The Good King. 148
Kickapoo Rose. 150
How Things Came to Be 154

Introduction

Curling was my introduction to the arcane side of Wisconsin life. It was nearly twenty years ago that a number of Columbia County neighbors led me to a long shed wherein heavy pieces of polished granite were shoved across a shuffleboard of ice while teammates swept the ice with brooms in advance of the stone.

"A gentleman's sport," said the realtor. "A test of mental skill and fine physical technique," said the banker. "As good excuse as any to get out of the house in winter and have a few glasses of brandy and swap stories," said the beef farmer.

It was this third informant whose cheery bluntness set this Pennsylvania native on the road to discovering the story wealth of my adopted state. Years of listening in kitchens, hunting shacks, ice shanties, bait shops, lumbermills, taverns, churches and sweat lodges introduced me to the rich mixture of Wisconsin folklore.

It does not take long to see that Wisconsin offers a unique blend of ethnic groups, obscure activities, and reverence for the land that makes for a great storytelling environment. The stories themselves are a cultural relief map of Wisconsin. A campfire story at Yellowstone Lake in Lafayette County may yield up a spooky pioneer tale, while a visit to an auto race on ice on Lake Superior might grant us an insight or two into the winter mindset of the Northwoods.

The first decade of my story collection efforts was spent soaking up random offerings: railroad lore, ghost stories, Northwoods legends, American Indian teachings, UFO sightings, and wild tales from the deer and fishing camps. Next came my first attempts to share these stories in the form of short articles for local historical societies. Finally, I published some of these stories in booklet collections on individual counties.

Along the way I learned that not all stories could be lumped into the folklore category. Some, including many American Indian oral traditions, perform sacred functions and yield spiritual truths. Those are not included here.

At the early stages, I viewed these oral traditions as an endangered species in our cultural heritage. I thought of the stories in the same way one might think about animals or plants that are teetering on the brink of extinction. I later learned that this view flows from an imperfect analogy.

Some older story forms are fragile and endangered. The ethnic identities, community settings, and folkway practices that mold them are fading away. In many areas of Wisconsin, the intergenerational transmission of this folk wisdom is breaking down. Folklore and storytelling are casualties of the same social trends that afflict stressed-out families.

On the other hand, there is a resurgence in the storytelling art and in the collection of oral history. Quirky and humorous stories find a ready audience. Local legends are as durable as ever. Expansive yarns are robust and thriving.

My friend Walt Bresette convinced me that contemporary storytellers understand their power. He told an astounded audience of environmentalists that the Ojibwe storytelling tradition justified the placement of a radioactive waste disposal site in northern Wisconsin. It must go somewhere, he reasoned, so why not in a place where stories will be told for thousands of years after today's states and nations are forgotten? The warnings within stories, he insisted, would endure long after physical markers had corroded or disappeared beneath debris.

A detour from conventional folklore took me into the realm of ghost stories. *Driftless Spirits: Ghosts of Southwest Wisconsin* resulted from this foray. The troves of ghost tales I discovered reinforced the lesson that many story traditions are alive and well.

The exposure to various story traditions helped broaden my view of folklore. It encouraged me to go beyond simply collecting stories and, in order to understand the content, to study the mythological and psychological foundation of storytelling.

My definitions of folklore and legitimate storytelling expanded to encompass all areas of human activity. I found as much meaning in an elderly woman's memory of preparing meals for a thirty-man threshing crew as I did in more classic stories of pioneer heroes.

I must confess, however, that I am particularly drawn to the types of stories included in this collection. I found Wisconsin in these stories: larger-than-life, cranky, independent, and exuberant.

As a physically large man raised in a family that appreciated strength and endurance, I had a natural affinity for the brawny heroes found in so many Wisconsin stories. My fascination with the human attraction to odd phenomena was fed by stories of strange creatures. Thirst for knowing was satisfied by stories of lessons of the spirit and the heart.

This collection draws upon all the above elements. All are included here under the tall tales label because they share the traits of exaggerated style and fantasy. Some possess a core of historical facts, but even those have been inflated through retelling.

The concept for this book took shape in discussions between Owen Coyle and me in the Foundry Bookstore in Mineral Point one pleasant Saturday afternoon in October. There, surrounded by maps of the old Wisconsin Territory, we developed a plan for a statewide illustrated collection of stories. Subsequent discussions in Pat and Mike's tavern in Dodgeville refined this plan into its final shape: A collection of Wisconsin "whoppers" about unsung heroes, unknown mythic creatures, and little-told parables.

The selection process began with a base of hundreds of anecdotes. Some were enigmatic, some obscure, and some profane. Those that were previously unpublished and primarily local were favored for inclusion here.

A collection of this nature must draw upon dozens, if not hundreds, of sources. Some were ships in the night, virtually tossing the stories over their shoulders on the way out the barroom door. Others cemented long friendships with the glue of fishing tips and general folk wisdom.

Just as important as the stories themselves were the guides to the sources. Many benefactors were part of the process of putting me in a position to "catch" these stories. Many others enabled me to hear a special Wisconsin cadence within the stories. A few even encouraged a presumption of understanding the stories.

I am especially indebted to those who have passed on: Bob Oberbeck, John Lawton, Don Hanaway, Tom Saunders, John Beaudin, Archie Mosay, Orlando Bell, Terry McDonald, Tony Hauser, Tiny Krueger, Sparky Waukau, George Vukelich, Erdman Pankow, and Earl McEssy. Sometimes one can hear a departed voice clearer than ever.

A story collector must also be nurtured by a precise combination of friendship, deftly timed pats on the back, kicks in the seat of the pants, and periodic resupplies of beer. Thanks to: Helen Loschnigg-Fox, John Bergum, Paul Gilk, Kathy Christensen, Steve Freese, Jim and Pam Wise, Joe Looby, George and Jane Siemon, Tom Gerber, Dean Connors, Sandy Bloomfield, Robert White, Frank Koehn, Roy Kubista, "Bear" Taylor, David Clarenbach, Jim Schlender, Pete Cody, Bob Larsen, Ed Huck, Marty Beil, Jo Stoll, Ted Ryan, Neil Giffey, Bill Hurrle, Bill and Ruth Hart, Walt Bresette, John Hess, Melva Phillips, Nettie Kingsley, Roxie Owens, Nick Meiers, Woody Welch, Jeff Peterson, Eldon Keeney, Jim Weikert, Dale Schultz, Bobby Bullet, Jim Chizek, Judy Borke, Len Stanislawski, Phil Neuenfeldt, Brian Rude, and Conrad Amenhauser. They may wonder how they contributed to this effort (and even disavow that they did), but contribute they did.

Conversational "buzz" in some of my favorite haunts contributed to my understanding of how Wisconsin stories are told. Thanks to the gangs at the Pier in Bayfield, Witz End in Stevens Point, Boyer Bluff on Washington Island, Reedsburg Office Supply, Turner Hall in Milwaukee, Baumgartner's in Monroe, the Dominican Community at Sinsinawa, Riki's in Mineral Point, Harmony Bar in Madison, Hooterville Inn in Blue Mounds, Water Street Saloon in Sauk City, Slaney's Inn in Lone Rock, Prairie Bookshop in Mt. Horeb, Bramble Press in Viroqua, Red Oak Books in La Crosse, the annual rendezvous at Villa Louis in Prairie du Chien, Life Tools of Green Bay, the Red Cliff Reservation of the Lake Superior Chippewa, the Ho-Chunk Historic Preservation Office in Black River Falls, the Kickapoo Co-op Exchange and Turkey Hill Orchards in Gays Mills, the Cranberry museum in Warrens, Pat and Mike's in Dodgeville, the Lac Vieux Desert boat landing, American Legion posts of Eau Claire, Superior, Dodgeville, and Three Lakes, and many local historical societies.

This collection is a collaborative effort. The collaboration dates back to 1980 when I joined Owen Coyle in the Wisconsin office of the American Federation of State, County, and Municipal Employees. Our capacity for mischief is considerable and will not be fully disclosed until after all applicable statutes of limitations expire and provide safety. Our partnership is proof that the world rightfully fears that the Irish and the Germans might get together. *¡Salud, amigo!*

Owen and I both extend our appreciation to publisher Jerry Minnich. His skillful guidance is appreciated.

A final word of thanks must go to my family. My wife, Donna Weikert, has steadfastly supported my late-blooming writing ventures. My sons Sam and Ben egg me on with their constant calls: "Dad, read us a story."

All this support has enabled me to begin to understand how these smaller stories fit within the broader Wisconsin story and the global human story. The kindness shown to me has aided the search for meaning, light, and laughter.

Dennis Boyer
April 1, 1997
Town of Linden
Iowa County, Wisconsin

PART ONE

Heroes and Rogues—
Larger than Life Characters

Badger Bill

Southwest Wisconsin is rich with European American folklore. No other area of the state had such an early mixture of trappers, traders, miners, loggers, boatmen, and farmers. Throw in the unique topography, the frothy mixture of European immigrants and old eastern stock, and the echoes of the Black Hawk War, and you have fertile compost for story growing.

The region produced the first unhyphenated American stories in Wisconsin. It went past the European motifs of La Baye, Fort Howard, La Pointe, Madeline Island and Prairie du Chien. It produced stories shared by New Englanders, Southerners, and recent immigrants.

Sometimes too much is made of melting pot theories and too much effort is wasted on homogenized American folklore. Most folklore is local and rooted deeply in ethnic, national, and religious groups.

But the rigors of constructing new lives and new institutions on the frontier created space for merger and exchange of oral traditions. The early one-room schools and intermarriage were vehicles for gradual synthesis. So were the male domains of commerce and industry.

Lead mining, lead processing, and lead trading were the primary seeds of this new American self-definition found in southwest Wisconsin. From the miners, a whole state drew an identity: Badgers. It was a plucky and tenacious identity that shaped politics and community life in ways felt right up to the present.

Much is made of the badger as the strutting mascot. But in southwest Wisconsin, almost every town had a human badger who served as a symbol of grit and determination. And sometimes one can find hints of overarching stories that serve the entire region and all its groups.

A stop at the Foundry Bookstore in Mineral Point often produces such leads and hints. There, among the stacks and drawers of rare books and maps, one finds clues to Wisconsin's past. The inventory complements conversation with the eclectic mix of customers.

Clarence, a businessman from Darlington, is a frequent visitor to the stacks. His Wisconsin roots go back to a trader ancestor in Lafayette County in 1828. His American roots extend back to the late 1600s. He chuckles as he begins to explain the meaning behind the American and Wisconsin stories.

Badger Bill is as Wisconsin as a slice of cheddar! Badger Bill is every American hero. He is John Henry, Casey Jones, and Paul Bunyan. He is American in the sense that his essence is right off Bunker Hill and Valley Forge. He is European in the spirit that built awe-inspiring cathedrals and resisted feudal tyranny.

He belongs to all the groups and none of them because he represents an emerging young state with its own niche to carve. If you checked his bloodline, you would find that he is half Cornish. But you'd also find Welsh, German, Norwegian, and Scotch-Irish branches on that family tree. Check back a bit further and you will discover roots in French Canada, Vermont, and Virginia. And somewhere on the mother's, mother's, mother's side—a dash of Ho-Chunk blood.

Depending on who tells you the story, you will find Badger Bill in almost every time frame from the earliest pioneer days right up to the end of mining. Because of that, I tend to think of Bill Senior, Bill Junior, and Bill the Third.

How else can you reconcile stories that talk about Bill fighting as a private in the Black Hawk War and the Civil War? How else can you compare stories that place him in covered wagons, old steam trains, and trucks?

There are hundreds of Badger Bill stories. They include nearly every theme known in the annals of human determination and triumph. You have heard them in many forms before. Man wins the race honestly. Pluck and purity of heart lead to reward. Strength of character and physical strength make an unbeatable combination. Man triumphs over machine.

My favorite is "Badger Bill's Deep Mine." In it, Badger Bill finds lead where others have not. They say he dug the deepest mine over by Wiota. Like Noah with the ark, he took a lot of ridicule and abuse for continuing on with a seemingly futile task.

An old Indian man told Badger Bill that there would be a large lead deposit under a hill. He knew from his own experience that sometimes the lay of the land created pockets and veins of minerals at great depth.

All the other miners contented themselves to work the easy way to find ore near the surface. But it played out quickly and just as quickly the earnings were spent.

Badger Bill kept digging his tunnel. Every so often there was a speck of lead to let him know he was on the right track. The little bits of lead kept his spirits up.

Other miners tried to lure him away. Come to Linden, they would say. Or they would talk about a new site near Highland. Or they would brim over with excitement about gold and silver strikes out West.

Badger Bill would politely turn down their offers. He would repeat his belief that a man is fortunate to be allotted one fortune in his life and that he meant to claim his despite any inconvenience.

A tough Tennessee woman heard about Badger Bill and his deep and unproductive mine. She sought him out despite the warnings of friends and family. She explained that she wanted a man who knew his mind and could stick with things.

The two of them married. They seemed very happy with each other. But all the local people thought they were both crazy.

Then one day, Badger Bill struck the main ore body. It was the biggest lead deposit found up to that point. Badger Bill and the Tennessee woman became rich, and they and their children never wanted for anything.

I like the messages in there. Not only the simple perseverance and work ethic but more. Like not worrying about the opinions of those with little sense of direction. Like not settling for the short-term solution.

There is even the advice on finding the proper mate. Look for someone who embraces your traits and is committed to them. The Tennessee woman is the earthy and robust woman looking to share passion and adventure, not the dependent wallflower.

Then there is the deeper symbolism of the subconscious. The old Indian has the secret of the mine. The old Indian is the intuition and the connectedness to the signs that the Earth offers. Listening to the Indian is self-discovery.

The deep, deep mine is that sense of self. It is the soul of secret knowledge. By digging that shaft, you find the treasures within.

Badger Bill stories tell us a lot about our Wisconsin values. In a way, it is America's story, or at least we like to think so. America's story is not perfect. A lot of people were left out of it for a long time and still do not share fully in it.

5

It is as easy to misinterpret Badger Bill as it is to draw conclusions from the American story. There are those who see these solely as rugged-individual, pull-yourself-up-by-the-bootstraps stories.

Well, they are wrong. That counter-myth is a virtual paid political advertisement for emotionally dead success chasers. That kind is as un-American as they come.

A Badger Bill story always has a *social* context. There is always a loyal partner, a spouse, a family, or a community. His strength serves others and he gets their support.

It is really the same as the Abe Lincoln story. A real American hero moves men's hearts to sacrifice and betterment. He is greater than us but not distant from us.

A real hero is fully engaged. A "dirty Harry" cynically plods through the wreckage. A real hero can be found at the head of a risky struggle. A junk bond trader can be found on a heavily guarded private island.

Badger Bill is the Wisconsin paradox. He loves nature and is steeped in the land ethic. Yet, he is also a tinkerer, an inventor, an entrepreneur, and a civic activist.

He blends progressive and conservative instincts in wholly unpredictable and imaginative ways. He has a keen eye for justice, an open heart, and is not quick to judge others. He is fiercely independent and still places the common good above his mere convenience.

Badger Bill is a good place to start a quest for the soul of Wisconsin within stories. Look for stories that help you understand the Wisconsin journey. It is more than words and symbolic meanings. It is about people in a place that changed them.

Find those places! Somewhere in a little town or backwoods cabin, you will find Badger Bill's spirit. You may even find him.

Langlade's Wild Boy

The feral child is a recurrent folklore theme in almost all cultures. Like Romulus and Remus, such children can represent the need to break from old cultures before founding new ones. Or, like Tarzan, they can represent our yearnings to escape society's conventions and to live the life of the noble savage.

In Wisconsin, the feral child usually is connected to the hardships of homesteading and poor survival decisions by parents. Such tales often contain references to themes of winter tragedy: burning cabins, death by exposure, and winter madness.

Somehow, a small child manages to survive. This survival is almost always linked to a nonhuman guardian. Wolves and bears are the most common agents.

But one can hear of other surrogate parents. In Vilas County, it is a lynx or bobcat. Among certain of the Ojibwe, it can be martens or fishers. Down in the old lead-mining district of Lafayette County, a pioneer tale revolves around the badger. In Sawyer County, it is a ghost or spirit guardian.

Wisconsin has at least a dozen feral child stories. They are old stories. The tone and content are invariably pre-twentieth century.

Except for Langlade's Wild Boy. There, a family at Parrish, in the northwest corner of the county, talks about contemporary sightings. Let Neil, the current story custodian, fill you in.

🌿 🌿 🌿

The Wild Boy is still roaming the Prairie River country, but he can be seen as far south as Ormsby. And fishermen have seen him clean over to Oconto County.

You gotta understand this is at least the fourth wild boy. By that I mean that our Wild Boy is at least the fourth generation.

Each of the earlier ones lived only to their early twenties. It's either their genes or the hard outdoor life. Our current guy is in his late teens.

Although he's wild, strong, and fierce, I've never heard of any harm coming out of him. One bad winter I think he may have taken some food. Oh yeah, he also dealt pretty harshly with a poacher shining deer over by Bogus Swamp.

He's quite a hunter himself though. He blends in enough to take deer without a weapon. I saw him when I was bow hunting in my tree stand near Payne Spring. The Wild Boy was able to get right alongside a nice doe. He slipped his hand around it and cracked its neck.

He fishes by hand, almost like a bear. I've seen him slap fish right out of the water. But more often than not, he grabs them out of holes in the bank.

He's a wiry fellow. He can run like a deer. He often plays with the bears and flips them like dolls. But they let him do it, of course.

He dresses in buckskins or furs, depending on the season. In the summers, it's just a deerskin loincloth. And he kind of hangs out of that, if you catch my drift. In winter, he's in a bear robe.

We have a family connection. He's a cousin, half brother or nephew or something. Maybe all those things. We've had some cousins marry in my family. Not that I'm proud of it.

But with the Wild Boy, there's a double connection. All the generations we know of had mothers in our family. It's nothing new in our family for a young woman to get pregnant without the benefit of marriage.

My sister gave birth to the Wild Boy that we've got today. She was only seventeen. That was nearly twenty years ago.

She died in a car wreck when the child was three. Mom took care of the boy for a while. But eventually, he just wandered off into the woods to be with his father.

We haven't figured out what happens when the fathers die. We never find bodies. Do the boys bury them or throw them in a lake?

Some say that the Wild Boy can communicate with animals, that he can get them to respond to his commands.

But I've never seen anything dramatic. I mean, it's not like he can stop an elephant stampede in Summit Lake or call the apes out of the Carlsen Road Marsh. That's stuff from old movies.

But I have seen him whistle up hawks, eagles, and ospreys. They come sit nearby him. And they'll even bring him rabbits and fish.

The only other stories I've heard about him have to do with his visits with the ladies. I've overheard such stories when the women's card group plays up at our house on Thursday nights.

Even though there's been a tradition of the girls in my family bearing the children, there's plenty to suggest that each wild boy visited many local women. I know one younger widow who leaves her windows unlocked for him year-round. Several generations back, a pastor's wife was known to take evening walks to meet him.

You might as well forget about trying to find where he lives. He won't let himself be followed home. He'll lead you around in swamps until you're lost.

In the summer, you might find an abandoned lean-to that he inhabited several weeks before. But in the winter, he finds the warmth of the bear dens of his animal cousins.

Iron Lena and the Ladies from Hades

Prudish Victorian values greatly restricted subject matter in the early phases of folklore collecting, and academics usually omitted many earthy legends and tales, particularly in the area of brothel lore. Such lore includes many cultural observations about the patrons, employees, and management of those facilities.

Three of Wisconsin's major activities were associated with brothel lore: mining, logging, and the northern hunting camps. Only the deer camp continued into the post-World War Two era.

One can chart the development and settlement of Wisconsin through the evolution of brothel lore. A brothel story usually represents a community at its most rough-and-tumble phase.

These stories were an almost exclusively male domain. The brothel madams who may have first told them have long since passed away or reformed. These stories were kept alive through retelling at shivarees (noisy and rude celebrations beneath the bedroom windows

9

of newlyweds) and later at "smokers" and bachelor parties. It was not a tradition of "family values."

Most of these tales are specific in location and time. This one—told by Rolf, a bartender in Spring Green—is exceptional in its geographical and chronological span.

🌿 🌿 🌿

It all started right here on the Wisconsin River.

Iron Lena set up shop across the river from old Helena and the shot tower. She was in business before Wisconsin statehood.

The exact date is kind of vague. Some say she was in the business at the time of the Black Hawk War. I doubt it. She was Norwegian and mostly they didn't come until the 1840s and 1850s.

She was a widow left high and dry, but she had good business sense and found an unfilled niche in the economy. Her house of pleasure brought miners, trappers, and boatmen to the area.

Her biggest problem in the early years was to find a workforce. Women were scarce in those days. You can bet that she wasn't getting them out of finishing schools back east.

The employees she could get were a rough lot right from the get-go. A lot had criminal pasts. Murder and assault were the most common offenses. Quite a few were scarred up from knife fights. That's how Lena's girls came to be known as the Ladies from Hades.

She counted among her customers rascals and reprobates like River Rat Fred. But many politicians and even future governors took their leisure at Lena's facilities.

There was an official desire to cover up these things and keep them from being publicized. Of course, the newspaper reporters and editors of those days didn't want to spoil a good thing either.

So you always had code words for what Iron Lena and the Ladies from Hades were up to. There might be talk of ladies of the night or hurdy-gurdy girls. Or you might hear of the pleasure palace, soiled doves, fancy house, and painted pigeons.

Rarely was there honesty about the real core of Iron Lena's business. There was just talk about the music, drinks, and entertainment. But I do remember my great uncle Ned showing me the site of the brothel and telling me that's where the early pioneers did the horizontal polka.

Ned claimed to have met Iron Lena in Hurley in the last stages of her career. He said his gang would come into Hurley from their Iron County deer camp.

He said she was quite educated and philosophical. She made it sound like her business provided psychological counseling and physical therapy. Kind of a respite from family, community, and business obligations. She was offering the illusion of the exotic.

She understood that pioneer and backwoods wives were used like draft animals. She understood what drab existence and the rigors of frequent childbirth did to those wives. She rationalized her business by looking at it as a way for rough men to blow off steam.

But I got ahead of myself. She didn't go straight from the river to Hurley. She made many moves.

Some say she moved the Ladies from Hades to Camp Randall during the Civil War. Some even think they followed the Wisconsin troops on the Tennessee campaigns.

After that, she apparently followed the logging business. First up the Pine River in Richland County. Then to Black River Falls. Later to Merrill and Antigo.

Ned said that she was on hand for the end of the white pine era in Ashland. Then she just switched over to the mine activity in Hurley.

You find that the legend leads places where there aren't always facts to back it up. Like that she was in Peshtigo during the great fire and lost a brothel full of artwork and French furnishings. Or that she was part of the gangster era at Little Bohemia at Manitowish Waters and dabbled in bootlegging.

One tale even puts her around Eagle River in the 1940s, supposedly still serving deer camp patrons.

11

This report leads me to suspect that there was really an Iron Lena Junior. If you believe all the stories, she ran brothels for about a hundred years.

Now, to my way to thinking, you can only look at this as a multigenerational thing or as a supernatural thing. Either daughters and even granddaughters kept the business going. Or she was like those old crones of the myths who could cast spells. Take it from a bartender, dim light and make-up can fool you.

She was known for prodigious feats of seduction. She was known to count her conquests not in numbers of individuals but in accumulated miles.

She is credited with having invented many of the toys and appliances delicately referred to in matchbook covers as "marital aids." But she may have gotten most of those ideas from a Chinese gal in her employ.

She had a rough life, what with moving around so much. But I don't think she was run out of many towns like you would suspect.

The old story about the Richland County Lutheran pastor sort of sums it up. A new schoolmaster comes to Richland County after the Civil War, to teach in a rough cabin school. At the annual school meeting, the teacher takes the pastor aside and tells him he is aghast to learn there is a local brothel.

The pastor denies that there is a brothel. But because the teacher suspects the pastor is naive and doesn't speak good English he persists. Is there a bordello? A fancy house? A cathouse? Finally, in frustration he explains the acts that offend him.

The pastor's eyes widen in recognition. "Oh, you mean the whorehouse," he said. "They have the best pie around over by that place."

Rewey's "Scotch Giant"

Heroes are always mixtures of history and legend. Admirers often show more affinity for myth than reality.

It often is the case that heroes lead dual lives. Many North American heroes arise from dull and humdrum existences and come to prominence through acts that confirm public belief that "the common man" is capable of extraordinary acts.

Sometimes a hero has a secret side that is even more fantastic than his public persona. Such is the case with the Scotch Giant, who is an acknowledged historical figure.

Let a Cornish family historian share his detective work with you while he sips beer in Rewey's lone tavern.

🌿 🌿 🌿

The "Scotch Giant" story is completely misunderstood by the public.

First off, he wasn't Scotch. He was Cornish as they come. And his name was F. W. Shadick. The Scotch business was simply a stage name. Shadick performed in circuses and exhibitions all over the U.S. and Europe and some say in other parts of the world too.

His connection to the circus is one of the few things people agree on. But some say he was a "strong man," some a "fat man," and some say he worked with draft horses and elephants.

The strong man idea is closest. When I was doing the family history—Shadick was an in-law—an uncle told me he saw a circus poster that showed Shadick holding up a shetland pony as you might hold a terrier.

As a local boy, he was called the Cornish Hercules. He worked locally as a teamster. He grew to seven feet four inches and three hundred seventy pounds.

His feats of strength were talked about for generations. He held up loaded wagons while companions would change a wheel. He physically restrained cattle.

At a younger age his drinking was legendary too. He was a regular on the Cornish tavern dialect-singing circuit. But he turned to the temperance movement later in life.

He was like those other drinking and singing Cornish. They could never say the letter *h*. So things like "have a helpful heart and hand" always came out "'ave a 'elpful 'art 'n' 'and."

But it was never his circus tours or performing for Queen Victoria that fascinated me. No, it's his secret side that gets my juices flowing. I love a good mystery.

All the evidence suggests that he was some kind of secret agent. Probably for the treasury department, but maybe for the army.

The uncle I mentioned had writings in Shadick's hand that described international bankers and black marketeers in Europe and sketched Japanese, German, and Russian ships in the harbors of Hong Kong and Lisbon.

Shadick often told the story of visiting the big cannon emplacements at the Straits of Bosphorus and of viewing Gibraltar and Malta through telescopes. He would entertain children in Rewey, Mifflin, and Belmont with stories of Italian counterfeiters, Algerian thieves, Malayan pirates, and white slavers in Arabia.

He always spoke from first-hand experience, according to the old-timers. He'd say things like . . . "then the Sultan threw me the sword and I split the would-be assassin in two." Now some of this might have been exaggeration. But much of it must have been truth.

It's not only the letters and drawings that make me think so. No, there's more. There's the comings and goings of visitors to Belmont and Rewey. Government men came to see Shadick all the time. So did foreigners. Then he would sometimes disappear with them.

He was probably what today would be called a hit man. His travels, particularly abroad, were often at the same time of accidental deaths of prominent people. Remember, we're talking about someone who could easily break a bull's neck with his hands or crush a man's ribs with his arms.

Don't get me wrong. I'm not for violence. But I don't think Shadick was a criminal. No, he was battling international criminals.

He had such a reputation as a good man. He was often cited for bravery and rescues.

This happened so much in reality that he was often credited with acts of heroism in events he could not possibly have been involved in. Stories have him at both the Chicago Fire and the Pestigo Fire, even though those great conflagrations happened on the same day. And he was also connected to the big circus train wreck at Leslie outside of Belmont, even though he was out of the country.

15

In the end, the stories of his death show the same confusion and contradiction. There's a fight over where he's buried.

We're ninety-nine percent sure he's buried here in Rewey. That's from records and people's memories. Yet Belmont lays claim to him and some over there say he and his wife are buried in that town.

The circumstances of his death are also mysterious. He was, of course, an eater of gigantic proportions. So there is some thought that he died after a massive meal.

It was nothing for him to eat a whole roast goose, wash it down with a gallon of beer, then polish off a whole pie. But he was given to eating contests. And he often took sick after these even though he was always victorious. Probably ulcers and gout.

When he died there was no mention of an eating contest. I find that odd. There was the nagging suspicion that he was poisoned. He had just received a gift of Spanish wine.

The strangest rumor surfaced after his death. Someone from Mineral Point glimpsed him in a Chicago hotel. Inquiries produced a story of twins separated at birth.

There were two Scotch Giants!

Dirty Pierre

Scoundrels *seldom achieve permanent status within folklore. Scalawags, reavers, grifters, bullies, and assorted other ne'er-do-wells usually serve as the foils in stories about more heroic figures.*

Some rascals manage, through luck or skill, to mold their reputations in the style of Robin Hood. But a few revel in their offensiveness and sociopathy. Sometimes their communities join them in the celebration of dastardliness.

The passage of time, of course, makes it easier to romanticize scoundrels. The humor in their disruptive deeds is easier to appreciate after the pain they caused has dissipated. Often the passing of the victims and the villains facilitates the transition from healing to laughter.

Many of Wisconsin's memorable tall-tale personalities have elements of the scoundrel to them. Skirting the law and defying authority are common themes. The skills of the con man and shady gambler are

frequent story elements. But usually a heart with some humanity, if not a heart of gold, beats beneath these nonconformist breasts. We have few irredeemable and irretrievable souls.

Douglas County has one such tale. It is as far as Wisconsinites care to go in canonizing no-account, shiftless, amoral lowlifes and still manage to chuckle about it. Perhaps a special twist in the story permits the laughter.

The story of Dirty Pierre is the best known tale in this collection. Most of the others circulate among a few or are genuine family heirlooms. With Dirty Pierre, I found almost a dozen informants who could add something to the story file.

It is not as if the account is on the lips of everyone in Superior. But some careful checking can turn up sources in the shadow of the Bong Bridge, on the docks of Barker Island, and around the old rail yards north of Belnap Street and west of Highway 35. Wisconsin chauvinism aside, the story also has some Minnesota roots, with mention in Duluth and Cloquet.

The abundance of sources made for a tough choice in picking a central narrator. The question was settled by a conversation in a tavern near the oil refinery on the south side of town. Sumner had a family tie to the story.

Are you really interested in a story about a no-good scumbag?

We just use it as a local joke. We might say that someone smells like Dirty Pierre or has the sticky fingers of a Dirty Pierre. Mostly, we're kidding around with a friend who knows the story.

Years ago, when the story was more widely known, the label was meant as an insult. To call a stranger Dirty Pierre was to guarantee a fight. It was a severe insult to one's honor.

Dirty Pierre was not representative of the pious French Canadians, the hard-working loggers from Quebec, or the sturdy voyageurs. In fact, the tale starts with Dirty Pierre being run out of Canada.

The time period is a bit hazy for me. I have the feeling that many of the events talked about in the stories happened in the era right after the Civil War. Things were pretty primitive up here at that time.

Then the logging boom hit. The Dirty Pierre stories fit into some of that history too. But you can tell he had worn out his welcome by then and was in hiding half of the time. By the turn of the century, the story ends.

The very first phase of the Dirty Pierre saga starts with his petty theft of food and belongings. He plundered everyone from isolated homesteaders to Indian agents to traders to missionaries. He worked the Lake Superior area from La Pointe to Grand Portage.

After a time, he came to focus on the Superior and Duluth area. It was handy for him because he could hop in his canoe and cross the St. Louis River to evade the law of one state or the other. Not that there was much law up here in those days.

He had a series of hiding places along Pokegama Bay and Clough Island. Little huts, caches of supplies, and rowboats hidden in the rushes. Some say there was even a cave or dugout on Dwights Point.

When more people came into the area, Dirty Pierre moved into phase two of his criminal activity. He sold bogus quitclaim deeds to gullible immigrant homesteaders. He even clipped a few logger company agents on phony timber sales on land where he had no legal interest.

Next, the area got a little more settled and he could diversify even more. He found all sorts of business swindles to engage in. One was called the revolving whiskey swindle because he sold the same barrels of whiskey again and again. He simply stole them back under cover of darkness.

But there were always supply contracts where the uninsured cargoes "fell overboard" in Superior Bay. There were company charter frauds where well-dressed co-conspirators sold worthless stock in nonexistent railroad, dock, and lumber companies. And there were the all-night card games where he fleeced the locals by use of trick mirrors, drugged drinks, and painted floozies.

By the height of the lumber boom, he was functioning as a loan shark, protection racketeer, smuggler, cargo hijacker, raider of Indian agency resources, pilferer of missionary funds, assassin-for-hire, bookie, and brothel owner. He was a one-man mafia, a one-man crime wave.

As bad as all that stuff sounds, he might have gotten away with those things. He might have been thought of simply as an enterprising boom town businessman. But no, like all tragic figures, he overreached. I guess he just had to see how much he could get away with.

So in the final phase, it was pretty seamy stuff. A string of unwed pregnancies, virtually all of them with underage girls. And some seductions of local prominent women that led to some pretty shocking Victorian era pornography. He was apparently slipping them opiates.

I guess it got to the point where half of the kids in town looked like Dirty Pierre. That was a scary thing on account of the gene pool and on account of his less than handsome looks. He had what they call a rat face and stringy, greasy hair.

It was these goings-on that finally did him in. It was the despoiling of the girls and ladies, the corruption of the youth, and the mockery of all decent values. And the town turned on him.

After all, he was the ultimate deadbeat dad, a Rasputin of the flesh, and a human predator in league with the Devil. So a large citizen group—which included my granddad—formed to hunt him down.

It took them awhile. He was a slippery cuss. And he had all those hideouts. He kept moving back and forth between Wisconsin and Minnesota. He even hid out over at the Fond du Lac Reservation in Minnesota, but the Chippewa ran him out of there too.

Finally a posse of about twenty young men cornered him out on Chases Point. They surrounded him and captured him. They trussed him up while they discussed his fate.

I guess even at the end, he was trying to weasel out of things. Trying to bribe them. Promising to show them hidden treasures on Clough Island.

But it didn't work. They strung him up in a big old basswood at the end of Chases Point. After that comes the disagreement. Some say the young men burned the body. Some say they weighted it down and sank it in Spirit Lake.

But it must have been quite a jolt to old Dirty Pierre. To see the hate in those twenty or so young faces. To look in their beady dark eyes. To see their chinless faces and drooping long noses. To know that a gang of his illegitimate sons had come to lynch him.

River Rat Fred

Bait shops and boat landings along the Wisconsin River are the oral history "libraries" for much river lore.

This tale may be a local variation on Mike Fink, the Paul Bunyan of the Ohio River, but it bears a distinct Wisconsin stamp.

Lamont, our source here, knows the Wisconsin River from Sauk City to the Mississippi like the back of his hand.

🌱 🌱 🌱

Ah, rivermen are the best!

The rest are just flatlanders, hillbillies, and bohunks. My granddad knew the best of the best. That was River Rat Fred. Now, there was a riverman.

The River Rat had arms like a Clydesdale's legs. He had hands that could squeeze your head like it was a lemon. Heck, Granddad saw old Fred squeeze a snapping turtle out of its shell with one hand.

Old Fred knew boats. Everything from sailing craft to the big grain boats. Once, on a bet, he paddled all the way to St. Louis on a haystack. He could sail a two-bottom plow if he had to.

Everybody in the river towns knew the River Rat. He had a wife and a couple of kids in every town from Portage to Rock Island. And they all loved him.

Granddad said we can be proud that old Fred called Iowa County home. He held the record for the most Iowa County residences: twenty-two in forty years.

You might say he had the first mobile home. Or maybe the first houseboat. He claimed a house brought down from Columbia County by a big spring flood. No dam upstream in those days.

Well, the house beached itself on the island just upstream from where Blue Mounds Creek empties into the Wisconsin. Old Fred just moved right in and set up housekeeping. He said there was still a warm pie in the oven from its prior occupants. He ate the pie and slept in a big featherbed for the first time in his life.

The house moved a little each time there was a flood. But old Fred didn't mind. He made a rudder for the house out of an eighty-foot white pine and a barn roof and just steered for the Iowa County side. That's because the Sauk County treasurer said he would levy a property tax if the house got stuck on the north shore.

That's how it went for forty years, the house slowly bumping from island to sandbar, heading west. Then he finally passed out of Iowa County when a big soaker pushed him over to the Town of Orion in Richland County.

While the old River Rat lived in his floating house he was king of the Wisconsin River. Every river bum, card shark, and trapper from

Merrill on down to Prairie du Chien came to pay homage at the castle in the river.

It was one hell of a foot-stomping devil's hoedown type of a place. They say governors and generals dined on deluxe catfish there. Maybe even a president or two.

Anyway, it was Fred's base of operations for his little empire. He *was* the law from Mazomanie to Blue River. No village board or banker made a move without consulting him. And within his domain he exacted tribute like a barbary pirate.

But he liked his fun, too. Couldn't resist a dare, bet, or contest. I think the best feat of river skill was when he rowed a flatboat from Prairie du Chien to Arena. Twenty-one hours straight into an east wind and rising flood. Right up a river chock full of stumps, bridge beams, dead cows, and bear turds from up north. All on a bet.

Another time he won the contest for the biggest fish a man could catch in his teeth. No false choppers allowed. Everyone thought the contest was over when a Winnebago woman from the Dells came up out of the water with a twelve-pound walleye between her teeth. But old Fred just took a gulp of air and dove to the bottom. This contest was just off the back porch of his river castle.

He came up with a ninety-pound channel cat. That catfish was so embarrassed that it begged everybody's pardon and went in the house, skun hisself, and fried hisself in the pan. Darn thing fed a hundred people.

When the tavernkeeper at old Helena bet a barrel of beer that old Fred couldn't cross the river during a flood, well, the River Rat was unfazed. He whistled a special whistle and every muskrat, mink, otter, and beaver within twenty miles came and created a fur bridge for old Fred to walk across.

Then there was the contest to see who could catch the most snappers. After a half day, old Fred came back with a hundred and fifty-eight all tied in a line pulling his canoe like huskies pulling a sled.

That's how it went for forty years until the house floated out of Iowa County. Over in Richland County the temperance ladies brought the law down on him.

But in a few years he escaped them. A big flood swept the house and Fred right down the Wisconsin, down the Mississippi and out to sea.

Last anybody heard he sailed that house around the world. It was one of the first vessels through the Panama Canal.

The Hiding Kickapoo

American Indian folk tales are as common in southwest Wisconsin as rock outcroppings. Pick a tribe: Ho-Chunk, Potawatomi, Sac, Fox, Kickapoo, or Iowa. The marks of all these groups are easy to find in artifacts and stories.

Many of the stories involve pioneer interactions with these tribes. Some focus on ancient legends. A few even provide insight about the extent of American Indian intermarriage with European Americans. The tale of the Hiding Kickapoo is different from these standard stories in that it involves contemporary sightings of someone attempting to live the traditional American Indian lifestyle.

Relationships between American Indians and European Americans in Wisconsin are weighted under the legacy of the Bad Axe Massacre and are colored by the current tussles over fish and casinos.

Cecil, a retired Crawford County highway worker, offers evidence of different attitudes as he tells his story at the Town Tap in Gays Mills.

🌿 🌿 🌿

Have you ever wondered what it would be like to go back to the way things were?

I often think about what it musta been like around here in 1820 or 1720. A different look to the land and different plants and animals.

It was back around 1981 when I got the first hint that maybe you could go back. That's when I first saw the Hiding Kickapoo.

I was driving patrol for the highway department up in this end of the county. I had Highway 131, Highway 171, a bunch of the county trunks. I coulda hit the fellow with my truck. It was foggy and he ran out of the old logging road that connects Bown Road and Highway 131.

Yeah, he ran out right where that trail empties onto Highway 131. Just south of Mother Lot Point. He sure scared me. Young fellow. Long black hair. Just some rags around his middle and his privates.

Now, my first thought wasn't about Indians. No, my first thought was "damn crazy hippy." I thought of those long hairs from the farm commune.

I saw him again about a year later, this time off of Pine Knob Road near County B. This time I could see he was Indian. Strong face features, thin, and wiry. And he was carrying a bow and arrow!

But I still didn't know what to make of it. I thought maybe it was just some young college-educated radical Indian fooling around in the summertime.

A couple more years went by and I heard things from other people. Things about Indians coming back into the area. Things about a group of Indians that hid on the Hogsback near Steuben.

But those things didn't have much to do with what I saw. Those reports mostly came from different medicine men who have been coming back to visit their sacred sites. And the Hogback stories probably came from an Indian clan that stayed in the area and married into the local families down there.

But by the mid-eighties I found out that I wasn't the only one seeing the young Indian man. One by one I heard bits and pieces of similar stories from Wauzeka up to Ontario in Vernon County.

A professor out of La Crosse looked me up. He was trying to put the pieces together. He had talked to five or six others who had similar experiences.

He was the one who educated me to the Kickapoo angle. Funny things about that, with the Kickapoo name all over around here. No one knows anything about them as a tribe.

They were a gypsy bunch. Moving here and there. More so than other tribes. They came through Wisconsin, got on the wrong side of a couple of wars, and got split up. Some ended up in Kansas, a small group in Washington State, and some across the border in Mexico. While they were around here for a while, they weren't long-time residents like the Winnebago. I guess this section didn't have any long-term settlements.

So you can see I learned a lot about Indians that I didn't know before. Borrowed a bunch of books and I wanta get some more.

Our feller here was identified on the basis of his arrows. The professor had one. I guess there was some other stuff that gave it away too. None of this tells us whether our Indian is a modern fellow who went back to his roots or one of those from down in Mexico who knew the old ways.

He was killing deer pretty regular with his handmade bow. He made his own fish traps too. Then there was tanning of hides, drying and smoking meats, and building shelters.

We've found his little bark huts that he makes during the summer. He moves a lot then. As far as winter goes, well, that's a little hard to say. We used to think he went south for the winter. But now I'm pretty sure he's holed up in a cave that time of year.

There was a time when some of the local young bloods thought they should hunt the Indian down. But some of us around here sorta got the word out to leave him alone or they'd be dealing with the business end of a twelve-gauge.

But the Indian fellow did more than we did to discourage foolishness. Guess he got two or three of them in the ass with arrows.

None of the old-timers had any contact with him. No howdy-dos, no talk about the weather. As far as we know, no one has talked to him.

But there is an interesting rumor. One of those commune gals would often run out to the woods at night. A little redhead who later got big in the belly.

It's lucky for him that he lives as he does. If it were a group, or even a family, we'd have all sorts of people tracking them down. This way it's more of a hazy story that can't be proved one way or another.

In the end the big question is why? Why here? Why now.

I think the answer is in some other questions. Why are we seeing wildcats around here? Why are the bears moving back? Why are we starting to hear panther cries and wolf howls in these hollows?

Maybe there's no one answer. Maybe we're going back in time. Maybe the abandoned farms and the grown-shut pastures have a good side to them. Maybe all those old homesteads sold to Chicago people who hardly ever come up give the land time to rest and heal.

All I know is that the Hiding Kickapoo needed us to change. I guess we are. I wonder what's next?

Wyalusing Snake Man

Snakes occupy a curious and long-standing niche in folklore. Fear, symbolic dreams, and weighty biblical references combine to create a sure-fire recipe for tall tales. Such tales usually run toward the sinister side, with occasional references to wisdom and endurance.

European American tales about snakes usually emphasize stealth and cunning. American Indian stories often cast the snake as a message bearer or tranformative agent (coming out of something or going into something). Both traditions seem to put snakes in a dialog with humans.

Stories about men who have mastered snakes are far rarer. They belong to that genre of stories that might be labeled "beastmasters." Venerable stories from Daniel in the Lion's Den to the Pied Piper of Hamlin could be included in that sturdy tradition. Saint Patrick of Ireland certainly could be assigned to this category.

Wisconsin's European American snake stories usually take a different tack from the European tales. Our stories tend to emphasize either ruthless elimination of snakes or snake humor.

Occasionally, one can find, as with the Wyalusing Snake Man, a combination of these elements.

I first encountered this tale in the early 1980s, not long after I began collecting folklore. It was included in a booklet entitled Tall Tales and Odd Characters in Grant County.

Subsequent story-collecting efforts enabled me to place this tale within a broader collective subconscious of southwest Wisconsin. Snakes are more common in southern Wisconsin and so are snake stories. But the highest density of snake stories can be found in the Wisconsin River valley from Sauk Prairie down to the Mississippi and in the Mississippi River valley from La Crosse south to the Illinois line.

Elements of the Wyalusing Snake Man can be found in many of those stories. Common threads are a high level of irreverence and a sing-songy, half-rhyming style. All of these stories bear marks betraying origins in the upper South.

Stan delights in telling this tale to children. A lifelong Bagley resident, he will perform in any Grant County hollow with a campfire, but he is at his best with his large flock of grandchildren and great-grandchildren. He stirs the sparks with a stick and tells the family legend.

🌿 🌿 🌿

Well . . . , is everybody ready to hear about the snake man?

Are you really ready freddy? Ready to crack a nut with your butt? Check under the rocks and lock the locks? Wouldn't you just hate if you sat on a snake?

Well . . . , thanks to my grandpap, you don't have to worry about them things that do scurry. Grandpap come up from the South with a dollar in his mouth. Rode a mule, he was no fool. It was too far to walk and, praise the Lord, the mule couldn't talk.

Grandpap came from Tennessee, you see. Or can you see? It's the home of seesaws, seabees, chicken-of-the-sea, and singing oh-say-can-you-see. It's where men are men and women are more so.

Grandpap was my grandfather on my monkey's uncle side. He kept the family history by tanning their hides. Shirttail cousin to everybody in these parts. He drove men crazy and stole ladies' hearts.

He was the infamous and famous, the notorious and glorious, the heroic and stoic Wyalusing Snake Man. My, my, in Wyalusing they had snakes in those days. Snakes in the fog. Snakes in the haze.

Snakes as big as utility poles. Snakes using mine shafts for their holes. Snakes as big as you'd ever want to grow. Living in herds like the old buffaloes.

They came down off the bluffs for a breakfast of barnyard dogs. Then after a belch they'd lunch on five hundred-pound hogs. What they et for supper I can't rightly say. 'Cause by then the people was hiding over in Ioway.

So we had snakes in those days. Snakes in the worst ways. Curling, squirming, slithering, sneaking, creeping, out-of-the-grass peeping snakes in all nine million varieties that the good Lord placed on this planet just to remind us who's boss.

But the Lord depends on us to trim the sails and work out the details. And details be known, there was just a mite too many snakes in this here Mississippi bluff country. Why, a man could hardly sleep at night for all the rattlesnake rattling.

But nobody knew what to do about it, except the Wyalusing Snake Man. He'd been a meat hunter for the Rebel Army in the War Between the States. He kept the Arkansas and Tennessee boys fed on lizard and snake meat. Snakes so big they had to be sectioned and shipped up on Texas railroad flatcars.

So he knew what to do. He knew a thing or twenty-two. And the thing he knew—faster than me or you—was that you need a big gun. Now he would have liked a fifty-pound field gun to load with grapeshot, but that's not what he got. No, the best they can do for that old son was a rusty and musty old buffalo gun.

So he loads the gun up with a sack of flour, ten kegs of nails, five anvils, and a barrel of gunpowder. When those snakes started down for breakfast he let the whole thing fly! Boom! By suppertime, everybody in Grant County was eating rattlesnake pie.

Everybody et and et snake. Canned it up in jars. Filled the smokehouses with snake hams. Lashed the really big snakes together like logs and rafted them down to New Orleans to sell to those fancy eating places. He was in charge of that, too. He ran off those Germans in St. Louie who wanted to make snake sausage.

Anyway, that took care of the really big rattlers, Grandpap held a meeting with the remaining snakes and laid down the law. No more dogs for breakfast and hogs for lunch. No more sheep and steer suppers with old maids for dessert.

He told them that from now on there'd be a five-foot limit on rattle-snakes. He put the bull snakes in charge and told them they could grow to ten foot.

But his work wasn't over. He wasn't living in clover. This man of no fear had just begun a long and profitable snake career.

First, he had to clean up all the big snake rattles left behind. He cut and sold them as round barns to any Norwegians he could find. But that move came with a cost for without any corners a Norwegian gets lost. Those Oles would still be in those barns I fear, if he hadn't burned them down and offered them a beer.

So Grandpap thunk and thunk and came up with a better notion. He got the idea from a picture from across the ocean. He thought those rattles as Russian and Greek church steeples would be pretty. Heck, you can still see them in nearly every city.

Grandpap really got cooking when they put in the rattlesnake bounty. Before it was a public service. Now it was a business and he could live off the county.

But the day came when the snakes were almost gone and that actually made Grandpap sad. To lose them all would definitely be bad. So a big change of heart is what he had and, you know, those slithering snakes sure were glad.

The Wyalusing Snake Man made his new friends part of a show. They were with him wherever he would go. Over in Ioway they made a special harness for a hundred-snake hitch, hauling a wagon so packed with crates you couldn't scratch an itch. And in those packed-tight crates were thousands and thousands of slithering snakes.

The snake wagon rolled into Bagley one day and, at first, people just wanted it to go away. But they bought the Snake Man's oil of snake 'cause they knew that this oil couldn't be fake. Milking snakes is a tough job for fools. You have to hire midgets and use custom-made little milking stools.

So the show rolled into Glen Haven and he stayed for a while. And darn if that money didn't grow in a pile. Soon his fame grew far and wide. So you know, he couldn't hide. Nope, nope, he couldn't stand still. There was nothing to do but join Buffalo Bill.

He played for kings and he played for queens. He went to some places where snakes had never been seen. Trained and groomed snakes working for pay. The Snake Man and his snakes starring on Broadway.

All things must end, this you must know. Even the Snake Man and the great snake show. Yeah, Grandpap passed on with a belch and a smile. But they sure gave him a send-off in the best snake style.

The train brought his body to Prairie du Chien or, as he called it, Dog Town. Everybody turned out to honor him from miles around. Crying and wailing, oh boy, was it rough. But the hundred-snake hitch pulled the hearse to the bluff.

A thousand people came to the funeral that day. Many gentlemen and ladies from far, far away. Speeches, a dinner, a preaching, and soft music from a band. All for Grandpap, the Wyalusing Snake Man.

Now he's dead and gone and that's true enough. But on moonlit nights he comes back to the bluff. So if you're good boys and girls we'll let you stay up late, and maybe, just maybe, you'll see old Grandpap riding a snake.

I seen him a time or two!

Picket Line Koski

Wisconsin's *larger-than-life characters are usually found in distinctly rural settings. The lives depicted are typically close to the Earth and are lived predominantly outdoors. Yet, it would be unusual if Wisconsin's progressive and activist traditions had not intersected with the turmoil of the cities' mills and factories to produce industrial folk heroes.*

If one looks hard enough, such heroes can be found. They are often partly "insider" tales told by master craftsmen. As a result, there are limits to the potential appeal to outsiders.

This story is unusual in that it crosses occupational lines and bespeaks a wider human solidarity.

Crowd in at the bar at a tavern on South 35th Street in Milwaukee. The bar shows the wear of generations of machinists, autoworkers, electrical workers, and steelworkers. The walls are lacquered with the smoke of hundreds of railroad brotherhood meetings.

Listen to Milo, a retired welder on the stool down in the corner.

🌿 🌿 🌿

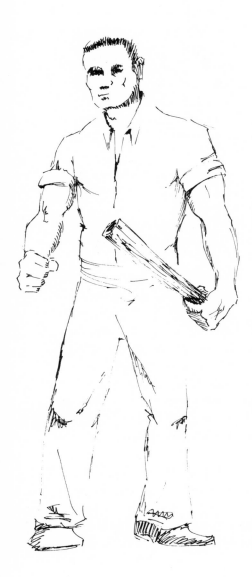

We need someone like that great son of the South Side.

There was a time when men fought for themselves and their families. And out of those fights there came natural leaders. Ours was Picket Line Koski. He earned the name on picket lines. Usually his fists up or on some scab's nose.

He wasn't a tall man. But he was powerfully built. Wide chest and large hands. A bit dark to begin with but with plenty of grease and cinders ground in.

Koski was born in Poland. He was a veteran of the Prussian army at fourteen years of age. He helped form and drill the Kosciusko Guard when that outfit was Company B of the Milwaukee Militia.

So he had exactly the experience you'd want in an organizer and a fighter. He understood discipline and he understood sticking up for your buddies.

He first appeared on the scene during the big rail strike of 1877. He was just a young laborer then. But he proved himself by hopping moving trains and throwing the scab crews off.

By the time of the big movement for an eight-hour day, he had grown in skill and reputation. He was called all around the Midwest to help pull together the movement. Especially the Poles.

31

He would often speak to crowds of thousands of workers from atop a boxcar or trainyard water tower. He'd speak first in Polish, then German, and then English.

He didn't just talk about the eight-hour day. He threw himself into it body and soul and put his life on the line. He often waded into a whole pile of scabs or got surrounded by a squad of clubbing cops. When the dust cleared, he was always the last one standing.

He would have been a great union leader if the Haymarket bombings—and later the hangings—hadn't set back the movement at that time. He was an angry man coming out of that!

He operated in secret pretty much after that. But you could do that on the South Side. He was a first-class Pole and the people down here took care of him. He changed names and hid in people's attics.

The Poles were united at that point. There were seventy thousand Poles in Milwaukee in 1910. We had newspapers, clubs, and our own high school.

Then came World War One. Koski was on the side that said workers should fight bosses, not other workers. That got him into trouble with the church and the Polish community leaders.

So Koski was a hero to the socialists and the radicals. But the priests bad-mouthed him as they blessed the hundreds of South Side boys going off to fight in France.

That drove him out of Milwaukee for a while. He spent much of the 1920s with the Industrial Workers of the World—the Wobblies—out west.

Those were tough times. Union men mugged, beaten, and even lynched. Koski drove off many thugs in logging and copper-mining country with a heavy oak cane he started to carry at that age.

You might say his last hurrah was in the Great Depression. When the unemployed organizing committees were started, he was there. When the people got organized against the banks foreclosing on homes, he was there. He was there stirring up the bread lines and the soup kitchens.

So when the CIO hit Milwaukee in a big way, he was in his glory. Out on the picket lines again. Milwaukee, Racine, Kenosha, and West Allis. Even Sheboygan and Green Bay.

By now he was an old, old man. So he really couldn't bounce the scabs around anymore. But he still shamed them. Bumped bellies with the cops. Pulled the ears of the young punks and told them their Polish grandparents would be rolling in their graves.

But he boosted morale wherever he went. No picket line or union rally in Milwaukee's CIO days was complete without him. His presence gave people confidence.

There was some violent stuff in those days. Shootings on the picket lines. Bombings of factories and union halls. Bad stuff from Youngstown, to Flint, to Gary, to Minneapolis.

Some say Koski disappeared during all that. The businessmen said he blew himself up with a bomb. The CIO boys said the bosses had the mafia get rid of him.

But I know different. I saw him in England in 1943. He was training Polish Americans for missions in occupied Poland. The last I heard he took a group in personally by submarine.

After the war—in the strikes of the forties and fifties—he was our combination Kilroy and Joe Hill. We'd start rumors. "Koski's coming," we'd say. Or somebody would claim Koski showed up at the Allis Chalmers union meeting. Or down on the Allen-Bradley picket line.

You young guys could really use him right about now!

Milwaukee's Juju Mama

Wisconsin's African-American folklore is heavily tied to the Old South. Tales of slave hunters, the Underground Railroad, and the nightriders of the Reconstruction era followed the freedmen and runaway slaves to their new homes in the Dairy State.

Ironically, some of the oldest African-American stories are found in rural Wisconsin along the old escape routes. The urban tales are of more recent origin and relate to industrial settings.

Stories that harken back to African roots are harder to find. A few false leads sent me after exotic tales that turned out to be recent Caribbean imports. Other referrals introduced me to college campus stories that were clearly yarns from foreign students' homelands.

The story below caught my attention because of personal interests in folk medicine, ghost lore, and spirituality. It is a rare tale that involves all three elements.

Our source here maintains a cheerful mix of belief and humor about the story she tells. Her north side Milwaukee home is a small but tidy museum of religious artifacts.

Her African-American roots include an eclectic mix of freedmen Great Lakes ship builders, frontier buffalo soldiers, Mississippi sharecroppers, and longtime Milwaukee business people. Her age permits both warm memories of pre-Prohibition Milwaukee and grim recollections of Great Depression hardships. She connects her story to broader African-American currents within Milwaukee's diverse cultural mix.

❧ ❧ ❧

You don't hear much about the old African magic anymore.

It's hard to know how much was African anyway or what parts of Africa it came from. Some of the things were picked up by slaves from the Choctaw and the Creek Indians. Some of the medicine probably dates back to Arab traders in West Africa.

The church is strong in the black community. The church never cared much for the old magic. Preachers spoke out against it and many Christians avoided the conjurers, sorcerers, healers, and fortune tellers that we had years ago.

My family always had a more tolerant approach. What can it hurt? I mean if the same person wants to speak in tongues at the neighborhood church, light a candle with the Catholics, share a holiday with an old Jewish neighbor, and buy a Juju charm, what can it hurt? It's always a good idea to keep your options open.

Our family had good experiences with the old magic because of Aunt Lucille. She was the last of the Juju mamas. Real power, not like those fakes we have today. She helped with health, love, and prosperity. It was not an accident that we were able to get backing from those old tight-fisted German families.

My, my, even the big brewery families like Pabst would use her when their university doctors failed. She cured many a white child.

The Poles and the Italians used her too. But she didn't care much to go to their neighborhoods because of the cruel children and mean dogs.

She worked the full range of people's problems, not like some who would do a charm or two or cure one kind of disease. She had studied all the old magic.

As far as we know, she was the last complete and initiated great mistress of the Grand and Benevolent Order of Juju. She was a full granny doctor, conjurer, and seer. In other words, a Juju Mama.

She said that most of this magic came from Gambia. It was brought over by hooguns or priests. But in old slave culture, the men couldn't practice it and the women took it up.

You had to study for about ten years. After that, you can raise the dead, change shapes, perform spells, mix potions, make charms, and lift curses.

She had extensive powers. She could make spirits and demons do her bidding. She had special control over Erzally, Spirit of Lust. People came from Chicago and Detroit for love charms and potions.

The things she did about love caused scandals. The white folks used her too. It was common for white boys from the best families to come and ask for charms to break down their girlfriends' resistance. Old Lucille always did—for a price. And only after she had bewitched the boys and made them spend the night with her.

She wasn't much to look at. Skinny old gal in a crimson turban and a black robe. Cross-eyed and bad teeth. But she was able to control some of those white boys and keep them coming back for more. She used a special wine with a potion in it. My, my, did that have tongues wagging.

Lucille also specialized in communicating with the dead. Surviving relatives often used her. Sometimes to contact a spirit and sometimes to make one go away. Here she worked through old Sakabu, Lord of Darkness.

People especially came about their problems with revenants, returners from the dead. Lucille had different exorcisms for different types. For the spirits obsessed with the pain of their death, there was one thing. The ghosts of murderers had to be overwhelmed with a more powerful spirit. Vain ghosts had to be convinced that they were remembered. Then there were the dim-witted ghosts that didn't understand that they were dead.

But it wasn't just about magic. There was more to this then amulets and poultices for arthritis. More than spooky stuff. It was part of community building and economic development.

You wouldn't believe how many black businesses were started off Lucille's money. A young man with a good idea could always get a loan. A young widow could always get a referral to a cleaning job in the German mansions. The preachers always got help with that new furnace or roof for the church.

Some say she's still around. Some of the fortune tellers say she's reincarnated in them.

I remember a funeral, but it was very strange. Part jazz parade and part Mardi gras. Lucille painted gold and sitting in a big throne up on a delivery truck. Nobody knows where she's buried.

So maybe she's immortal. Or maybe she's a zombie who still walks our streets. Some say she's working on the crack and AIDS problems. I sure hope so.

Deer Camp Dick

The Northwoods deer camp is as much a part of Wisconsin as cheddar and Friday night fish fries. Like everything else in sporting activity, the role of the deer camp is changing along with families and hunting techniques.

Deer camps fall into various categories of size, comfort level, and type. They run from tiny cabins to imposing lodges. Some are manors controlled by family patriarchs, and others are mini-democracies collectively owned by shop floor buddies.

Some deer camps have been used by the same families since the last century. Generation after generation pass along initiation rites and outdoor lore and skills.

Almost every camp has its tales of hunting prowess. Memorable hunting experiences are often connected to one particular hunter—a long-departed grandfather, a robust uncle, or a hard-as-nails local guide. The stories are always larger than life.

In some areas of the Dairy State, the deer camps share a common story. In the upper reaches of Forest and Florence counties, we find Wisconsin's premier deer camp story, as told by Arnie, a construction worker.

❦ ❦ ❦

Deer Camp Dick was the best there ever was—the best hunter, the best woodsman, the best camp cook, the best card player, and the hardest drinker I ever laid eyes on.

He lived for deer season. It was the peak of his year. The rest of the time he trapped, cut firewood, and did odd jobs. But in deer season he was king.

Deer Camp Dick knew where the big bucks hid. He shot almost all the trophies you see in the bars and barbershops from Wabeno to Aurora to Alvin.

And what a shot he was. Three hundred yards in open iron sights wasn't nothing to him. He used a beat-up 1903 Springfield .30-06 that had brought down hundreds of deer—legal and illegal.

His shooting wasn't just the ordinary crack shot stuff. He could shoot like a billiard champion. He made bank shots by ricocheting bullets off rocks. I saw him bring down a fourteen-point buck on a three-rock cushion shot around a hill at a deer where he only estimated its location.

And I saw him make combination shots where he'd shot another hunter's .30-30 bullet in two so he could kill two deer at a time. Sometimes the deer would be fifty yards apart.

His woodsman skills were equal to his shooting. He often threw his knife to silently kill partridges. Sliced their heads right off without spooking the other game. He threw hatchets at archery targets with the same accuracy as the best bow hunters. And wood chopping, wood splitting—well, none better. He could wield two splitting mauls—one in each hand—at the same time.

Deer Camp Dick had a special way with animals too. He always said he asked animals to please provide themselves as his meals. And he thanked them when they did. He took some deer by slitting their throats and some just by cracking their necks with his bare hands.

His cooking was legendary. He roasted deer whole in an old logging wood-burning steam locomotive that he had set up at his Spread Eagle camp. His sauerkraut-baked-bean-peanut casserole was famous in the Northwoods. Famous for taste and the explosive gas it produced. Made the best fresh deer liver and onions I ever tasted.

On the card-playing score, there's a bit of controversy. It's true he almost always won. But it was almost unnatural since he could read minds and had such good instincts. It was almost like cheating, but not really. But we always liked the way he fleeced the city boys.

His drinking would put the mythic giants to shame. He drank his beer out of a milk pail and his brandy out of a pint jar. He never lost a drinking match, although he attended many funerals of his losing competitors. When he quit drinking for a month on a bet, the Rhinelander Brewery went belly up.

You young guys who never met him always ask what he looked like. There's this impression that he was one of those bushy-bearded lumberjacks in a plaid jacket. No way.

He was a barrel-chested man of medium height. Popeye forearms, spindly legs, a thick neck and a bald bullet-shaped head. Face with a huge grin and a sweeping handlebar moustache with the spread of the horns on a Texas longhorn.

His family background was hard to figure. Even Dick didn't know much. You had to go back five generations to identify a male ancestor. His mother and the three females before her in that maternal line were all illegitimate.

The women were all hard luck cases. At least one dance hall girl. One abandoned mail order bride. One boarding house cleaning girl. And his mother was a fourteen-year old abused by a group of loggers. He later avenged her by disposing of the loggers. But he always wondered which one was his father.

All his women ancestors were of mixed blood themselves. Things like Bohemian and Finnish or Belgian and Norwegian. His only known male ancestor was an old one-eyed French-Menominee half-breed by the name of Willy Bojo.

Deer Camp Dick had a fifty-year reign as the top hunter in these parts. Like most true champions, he retired on the top of his game. We held a big raffle to send him on a retirement trip.

He went up to Ontario and found a whole new bunch that needed to learn how to hunt. So he never did come back.

Poker Run Pete

Winter sports are key components of the Wisconsin identity. Significant amounts of Badger State lore draw upon cold weather themes. Tales range from auto racing on frozen Lake Superior, to skiing the fabled Birkebeiner, to ice fishing in shanty communities from Kenosha to Superior.

Dozens of subcultures cherish their particular winter tales. They might concern spearing sturgeon on Lake Winnebago or the late season bow hunt along the lower reaches of the Wisconsin River. They could focus on the cordial brandy sipping of the curling clubs, or on the rough and tumble of a pick-up game of hockey on a hastily cleared patch of lake ice.

Much of the nation marvels at these activities and their associated rituals. Even many an urban Wisconsinite venturing beyond his neighborhood is amazed at the sheer numbers of people outside—doing things.

It would be unproductive and foolish to anoint one outdoor activity or another as the supreme cold weather sport. Loyal partisans from ice sculptors to snow golfers would protest vehemently against such presumption. It is just as pointless to assert that any one winter activity has produced the singularly Wisconsin story.

Cultural and environmental factors, however, favor the propagation and preservation of stories in some sectors of society more than others. The trail-focused and tavern-based socializing of snowmobilers gives them a huge advantage in the storytelling realm.

Eric, a small-engine mechanic from Eagle River, tells us how the American romance with speed, danger, and technology comes into play in this winter pastime. Listen closely in a shop filled with revving all-terrain vehicles and sputtering chain saws.

Poker Run Pete is the one you want to hear about. He's the original air-grabber, snow broncobuster, and ice-veined powder-tread
driver. He's the original breed, not one of those surf-bum refugees in
a skin-tight, Day-Glo suit.

Snowmobiling is a big industry now. We got our snobs and our hot-
doggers now. But we started off as real basic Northwoods fun. We were
one of the few winter sports that had something for the whole family.

Nobody gives credit to the pioneers of the sport. We forget that
many of those early trailblazers came out of Wisconsin. And of those,
Poker Run Pete is almost the most durable living legend I ever heard of.

Poker Run Pete is not his real name. It's more like his title. In
snowmobiling circles, the name stands on its own, like "The Babe"
in baseball. Hell, it's as good as being whapped on the shoulders with
the Queen's oversize letter opener and being called "Sir."

Up here we know who he really is. He's one of us. He has friends
from Caribou, Maine, to Kodiak, Alaska. I can't think of anyone who
guided the sport more and still serves as a patron saint.

To understand his role, you gotta go back in time. He was a grease-
monkey kid who fooled around with Indian-brand motorcycles. It was
that mechanical aptitude and his World War Two experiences that made
him a trailblazer in this racket.

He fought the Japanese up in the Aleutians during the war. Learned
about mechanical performance in harsh conditions. He stayed in the
service for a while and taught at the first Arctic warfare school. That
was until he was booted out for complaining to Congress that the military was not ready to fight a polar war.

He pulled together a lot of the early experimental rigs. His ideas
reversed the thinking that snowmobiles should be plodding little bull-
dozers. He knew that speed was the ticket.

He came up with a lot of experimental stuff. He knew people
wanted part fighter plane, part Indy racer. It took things away from the
early cement-mixer feel. He made one with front wheels to race on
dry pavement. He made another with a jet engine to run on the big
lakes. Talk about something major between your legs.

He's not what you'd expect—not a flashy guy on an Arctic Cat
Thunder Cat. Nope, he's a quirky old duffer on a welded-together
machine with all sorts of gizmos sticking off of it.

No winterwear fashion plate either. He dresses like a cross between a World War One pilot and a member of a motorcycle gang. Instead of one of the modern spaceman head coverings, he wears a leather aviator's helmet, goggles, and scarf. Below that he's all black leather.

He's quite a sight as he blows by all the sports high-performance jobs on his old beater. Anyone with a brain knows enough to get out of his way.

But I shouldn't make it sound like Poker Run Pete is simply a motorhead snow jockey. He influenced snowmobile culture in a big way. Maybe for good and for bad during a time when there were only a handful of machines running on isolated town roads. He came up with the ideas of trail marking and grooming.

He helped build it into a sport for families and couples. That came right out of his strong sense of family. His wife was the love of his life. She rode with him for forty years. And she still rides with him. After she died he made a place for her ashes on his rig.

He started his boys when they were little. He made little machines for them. We didn't think about kids' safety back then. He lost the youngest to a fence collision.

He also helped build the idea of driving from tavern to tavern. He thought it was a good way for people to avoid cabin fever in the winter. If it helped the tourist business, so much the better. He's working on casino ride-ins now.

His name comes from being the father of the poker run. That's where you ride from tavern to tavern and get a card at each stop until you complete your poker hand. Of course, the side benefit is the drink or two at each stop.

We need a guy like Poker Run Pete to brush up our image. The twits down in Madison get their jock straps in their crack just because a couple of guys put themselves through thin lake ice or off bridges each winter. So we need our elder statesmen.

Poker Run Pete is our coalition builder. He knows all the paper company managers and tribal officials. And he hangs out with the conservationist crowd.

He tells us that we gotta become environmentalists. He says we better kiss up to the tree huggers so that we get our cut of the DNR pie. Besides, he thinks the eco-freaks are right on global warming.

He makes some convincing arguments. Better than the bird lovers. I mean who cares if the thermometer goes up and offs some clams or butterflies? But warmer winters, now that's serious!

This country's greatness comes from men like Poker Run Pete. Rugged individualists who keep government off our backs. Don't look for government handouts. And just you watch, he'll get us more state trails!

Trapper Tom

Outdoors themes are so abundant in Wisconsin lore that such activities as hunting and fishing could easily constitute separate collections. Such outdoors skills as herb and edible plant gathering and survival shelter construction are a bit more obscure.

Midway between those poles is the ancient art of trapping. Only a generation or two ago, Wisconsin could boast tens of thousands of active trappers. The knowledge base still exists, but it has been driven underground.

Attitudes toward wearing fur apparel and the treatment of animals have created a public relations problem for trappers. Few critics of trapping understand that both improved technology and evolving ethics have altered trapping practices for the better.

It is unfortunate when contemporary controversies obscure important parts of our collective past. It is not hyperbole to say that trapping was a major factor in shaping political and economic events in the upper Mississippi Valley and the Great Lakes region. In part of the 1600s, all of the 1700s, and a bit of the 1800s, trapping reigned supreme.

Fur was the North American equivalent of Latin America's gold. European, Middle Eastern, and Chinese markets clamored for the luxurious furs produced in the Northwoods climate. Fortunes rose, whole communities withered, wars were fought, and entire peoples relocated with the vagaries of the fur trade.

At the center of this commerce was the producer of the bounty: the trapper. His American heyday was in the time between the Lewis and Clark expedition and the 1880s, but the legends and lifestyle lived on in rural pockets from Maine to Louisiana to the Pacific Northwest.

In Wisconsin, trapper stories are told from Sandy Hook to Niagara to Port Wing. Typically, they are part of broader tall tales. It is common to find a trapper segment within the stories about heroic boatmen, hunters, loggers, and pioneers. The Wisconsin River valley from Merrill to Prairie du Chien is home to many such stories.

But this La Crosse County story is the only one I found devoted entirely to a trapper character. It comes from the heart of a man who remembers the Calvert-Maple Grove area before sprawl swallowed up the river shacks. The twinkle in Burton's eye and the weathered face suggest many a frosty morning spent "checking the line."

🌿 🌿 🌿

Trapper Tom was the best.

That's what I heard when I was a kid. And I packed steel jaws on my back for darn near fifty seasons. A trapper in a long line of trappers.

That's how it was for Trapper Tom too. Almost a hereditary thing there. It's hard to get into and hard to learn unless a relative takes you under his wing. And Trapper Tom came from one of the most distinguished non-Indian trapping families ever seen in North America.

His grandfather was the famous John Colter, just maybe the greatest white trapper that ever lived. His dad was half Crow on the mother's side and brought up by that tribe until the age of fourteen. His dad married a half-Kickapoo woman who had land in the area, supposedly on Goose Island. That's why Trapper Tom is connected to the La Crosse area and the Mississippi River.

The old duffers tell me that Trapper Tom was quite a sight. He kept that old-time trapper look right up to the end of his life. He wore a badger hat with the head still on it. His coat was made up of strips of fur from just about every critter you can think of, so it looked like up and down bars of wolf, lynx, bear, otter, coyote, beaver, and raccoon. Almost like a fur corduroy.

His pants were usually buckskin. Just plain old buckskin for trapping. But for socializing he had special buckskin britches with porcupine quill beading and fringes dangling with bear claws, ermine tails, and bobcat ears. His boots were laced-up moccasins with mink trim.

He carried two big Colt navy revolvers tucked in a calico sash around his waist. Also in the sash was a large bowie knife. In the top of his left boot was his skinning knife. In his right was a light fighting dagger.

He was not a big man. Probably about five eight, but compact and muscular—around one hundred and eighty pounds. Round face, broad nose, and two mountain lion scars down the right sides of his face.

You should know that when he was set up on Goose Island, young men came for miles around—even from other states—to see the old trapper and hear his stories. Yes, he was a yarn spinner who could put you modern folklorists to shame.

First, he had the franchise on all the classic John Colter stories. Stuff like the battles against the Blackfoot. The running naked in the desert. The hiding in the beaver lodges.

Then he had his dad's stories. Sharing turtle soup with old Black Hawk himself. Trapping beaver on the Yellowstone. Packing bear hides out of the Yukon. Jumping ice floes in Hudson Bay.

But his own were just as colorful. Tricking Russian traders up in Alaska. Working as a tracker on polar bear hunts. Serving as a scout for the Rough Riders in the Spanish-American War.

He had a permanent hair part and scar from a bullet graze down the center of this scalp. He loved to tell that story. That was from him and a Montana trapper taking turns shooting whiskey bottles off each other's head. Then he'd show a hairy tobacco pouch and claim that it was the Montana trapper's scalp.

You could say there were history lessons in those stories too. He knew how trapping and the fur trade fit into how the frontier was tamed. He knew how the Indian tribes were put into the middle of this and how it set off the tribes against each other. Iroquois pushing Ottawa, who crowd Potawatomi, who bump up against Sac and Chippewa moving and running into Sioux. A chain reaction that stretched from the St. Lawrence River to the Columbia River.

He knew how it fit into the first big commercial empires. Like John Jacob Astor's American Fur Company or the British Hudson Bay Company. And how that set the stage for the empires of steel, railroads, and oil.

You can't possibly realize how important it was for young men to hear such talk. Not just the adventurers and the big whoppers, but the actual teaching of skills. So while Trapper Tom might have been a bit flashy like a Buffalo Bill, he was also full of practical advice.

You might say that Goose Island was kind of a trapping training academy back then. Trapper Tom knew all the angles. He could trap with the modern steel traps, but he also knew the old techniques. He could trap with snares, deadfalls, and pits. He had snared deer and bear.

He knew tracking and reading animal signs. He knew scents, lures, and baits. He understood the mating habits, life cycles, and hibernation periods of the fur bearers.

When the conservation era came along, he also helped spread the word. Oh, he may have shaved the rules kind of tight on some practices. But he showed the early game wardens just how the violators got away with things. And he convinced the youngsters that old romantic days of endless harvest were over. He helped the youngsters understand the need to protect the resource.

People have no idea how important this was to the boys back then. Trapping back then was the same as a paper route or a job flipping burgers these days. Fur was the jingle in the pocket for those trips to the state fairs and those train excursions.

Checking the line was often a boy's first assigned responsibility outside of household chores. The before-dawn checking of the trap line was a way of experiencing the cold, dark world of the marshes and riverbanks at night. It was learning to walk through the brush by starlight.

Trapper Tom is just the fellow who set the standard on my section of river. But for generations—maybe thousands of years—there were similar figures in every rural society.

But things are different now. We don't want to know how sausage or leather is made. We live apart from nature and our predator role in it. So there's no Trapper Tom for us anymore. Maybe we'll never see such men again.

Walter the Warden

Law enforcement work has generated relatively few folk heroes. Perhaps the public's expectation of high ethical standards and courage from their peace officers creates a belief that heroism is commonplace in law enforcement work.

It could be that some aspects of modern law enforcement seem political and therefore controversial. Incidents involving brutality and corruption, however infrequent, act to tarnish the work of decent and hard-working officers.

It is ironic that our few law enforcement heroes arise out of the times and environments that also produce our Robin Hood-style outlaw heroes. This is a basic folklore storyline that runs through frontier towns of the American West to the Prohibition battles between the "untouchables" and rumrunners and up to today's urban conflicts.

That is the tension present in this story of a Wisconsin conservation warden. It represents the conflict between two classic Wisconsin archetypes: the stalwart protector of natural resources and the stealthy backwoodsman who lives off the land.

Our narrator here does not incorporate this dualism into his own attitudes. A retired warden himself, Joe staunchly defends strict enforcement of the natural resources laws.

The story is told at the MacKenzie Center near Poynette, to wildlife biology students. Afternoon lectures on the history of fish and game protection give way to informal dinner discussions of "old-time" conservation work.

☙ ☙ ☙

A forty-five caliber Colt used to be the main tool for conservation education.

I'm talking about the era of the big, hairy-chested wardens, the biggest and hairiest of whom was Walter the Warden. No last names, please. Walter put away a lot of violators during undercover work. We still protect his family.

Walter was from the old school. He didn't have a lot of formal education. A couple of conservation manuals, some Aldo Leopold books, and a copy of the Wisconsin Statutes.

But he had a quick mind and even quicker fists. He had been through a lot of close-quarter fighting and hand-to-hand combat. A cavalryman on the Mexican border at the age of fourteen. Then a scout and infiltrator in the Argonne Forest in the first big war.

It was when he came back from World War One that he resolved to be a warden. When he got back he found that his favorite fishing hole had been cleaned out by dynamiters who sold the fish on the Chicago market.

Walter started as a "special," the old name for our assistants and temporary helpers. The old wardens liked their specials on the brawny and brainless side. Walter qualified on the former and could fool the old-timers to thinking he was a little slow.

Walter made the fastest transition from special to full-fledged warden ever seen in the old Conservation Department. Just one action-packed year of getting shot, getting run over by a car, getting beaten and left for dead, and arresting ten years' worth of violators.

When the chief warden saw how Walter took this physical punishment, he immediately recommended Walter's promotion. Walter proceeded to cut a swath through violators and made himself into a legend.

Walter began the exploits that made him a hero. He took an axe in the head while making an arrest. He was thrown off a train. He was thrown unconscious off a Lake Michigan fishing boat. He was thrown off a smuggler's freighter on Lake Superior, after he was weighted down with rocks.

48

He was a natural in rounding up the deer shiners, walleye spearers, lake trout smugglers, and beaver poachers. He could smell a crook. But his other skills were just as important.

He could escape from rope and chains like a Houdini. He could shoot off a poacher's cigar at a quarter mile. And he could swim frigid lakes, live off raw fish, snowshoe fifty miles a day, and sleep outside at forty below.

Walter became the inspiration for all the names they called us wardens: brush cops and popple cops, jack pine sheriffs, bear turd marshals, the woods posse, the trout police, and plenty of unprintable names. He had the decency and professionalism of a Canadian Mountie and the stubbornness of a mule.

He was responsible for many of our conservation warden traditions. Like being called by other law enforcement agencies. Everything from helping a deputy sheriff calm down a family dispute to assisting an FBI agent capture gangsters.

And like the tradition of sending the toughest warden into the meanest warden-hating towns. Walter was the prototype for that. He tamed many a poacher town. In the hard times, you had towns where poachers were heroes. Towns where even ministers and storekeepers wanted the warden dead.

It usually took him only about six months. Six months of poachers being treated for concussions and cracked ribs. Six months of big .45-70 holes in poacher car radiators and poacher moonshine stills. After six months with Walter, most violators started to attend church regularly. Heck, he even recruited some of the worst violators as specials.

He was kind of fond of some of the violators. He liked to match wits with the smart ones. And he always helped the poor families of the dumb ones. He just didn't cut any of them any slack on jail time.

As a young special, I heard two stories about Walter that stand out in my memory. One was about the time he was shot seventeen times. The other was about when he was held captive by a deer meat ring.

Getting shot seventeen times did slow him down. He lost a week or ten days of time in the hospital. But he arrested the shooter, who was amazed at Walter's survival.

Walter seized the two guns he was shot with and looked them over. Then he told the shooter that if he expected to put a warden down for good he'd better forget about sissy guns like the .30-30.

When he was hostage of the Price County deer meat ring, they tortured him to find out who his informants were. But they couldn't break him.

Finally they threw six vicious weasels in a gunnysack and tied the bag over Walter's head. Those violators expected Walter's face to be chewed off. There was snarling and whining from in that bag. But when they lifted the bag off, all six weasels had their heads bitten off.

The other old wardens thought that Walter was just the right crossbreed. He was Polish-Norwegian-Bohemian-Belgian. Kind of a throwback to Ice Age times.

He was tough even as an old man. His vagueness about his age kept him off mandatory retirement. Finally, he disappeared while on undercover assignment.

He had that great love of nature and respect for law that is the essence of being a warden. He would sure knock heads of current polluters if he was around today. Let's carry on his work.

King of the Poachers

Deep affection for natural resources is an integral part of the Wisconsin character. Among our heroes are men like John Muir and Aldo Leopold. Within our folklore are outdoors people whose love of the land is the stuff of legends.

But as much as we idealize our leading conservationists, we also have a small soft spot for those free spirits who live outside the rules. Not the large-scale despoilers and exploiters, mind you, but the subsistence-style outdoorsmen who leave the land as they found it.

50

The authorities classify these subsistence actions as lawbreaking and label their perpetrators poachers. The term poacher, *of course, encompasses everyone from the greedy commercial meathunter, slaughtering wildlife on an industrial scale, to the seasonally employed single parent stocking the Christmas larder with a fat doe.*

Irony can be found in the wink and a nod that some professional wildlife protectors cast in the direction of this homespun second category. It often happens that professional conservationists know exactly who is living this lifestyle and nevertheless fail to apprehend them.

Roy, our storyteller, believes that a tie binds the subsistence poacher and the protector of wildlife. It could be called a grudging mutual respect, but it appears to have a much deeper dimension that involves a shared relationship with the land.

A reduction in the federal workforce brought this fiftyish fish and wildlife employee to the Wausaukee area in a second career as a small businessman. Wait for a break in the evening frog serenade from McCall Marsh and the story will unfold in the shadows of a screened-in gazebo.

❧ ❧ ❧

I knew the King of the Poachers. The best at his trade that I saw in nearly thirty years of brush copping. And I saw my share! The fishing gangs on the Great Lakes. The big deer rings. The protected species smugglers. Saw them all!

Mostly crooks, lowlifes, dim bulbs, and human trash. But every warden, agent, and investigator will tell you there's another kind out there. We don't like to talk about it in public, but some violators out there really aren't hardcore criminals.

Some you pity because of poverty or backward family circumstances. With others, you know that what they did was a temporary thing from unemployment or whatever. Then with a few, it's just an old way of life that's ingrained in them like instinct in a wolf.

Just like a wolf, they're going to take some deer. But you have to marvel at the beauty and skill of it and decide for yourself if they're really hurting anything.

That was the key to the King of the Poachers here in the Menominee and Peshtigo river country. He never took so much as to throw wildlife out of balance. And, more importantly, he never got so public that it made us look bad. Those are the poachers we can't abide—the ones who leave gut piles all over the country and brag it up in the tavern.

The King just pursued his life. Living off fish and game was what came natural to him. It's what his family did for generations.

We often heard of him when I worked on Lake Michigan. But we even heard of him when I worked the Mississippi refuges. That's what gets talked about when state wardens and federal agents sit down for coffee.

He mostly worked this border country up here. Mostly from Lac Vieux Desert down to the Oxbow east of here. But when opportunity arose, he'd poach from Ontario, Canada, down to Marquette County. He'd just shift with the temporary laboring jobs he'd pick up.

The King of the Poachers was a premier outdoorsman. Not just a skilled hunter and fisherman. Not just a crack shot and skilled woodsman. No, he had many other abilities. He could move silently through the woods like a shadow. He had a bottomless bag of tricks.

Like when he improvised extra-long skis out of saplings and gave a warden the slip by crossing Lake Noquebay on the thinnest ice. Or, like when he tricked an agent into watching a dummy in a rowboat while the real action was going on elsewhere.

It's not like anyone tried real hard. It was more like we watched him to learn. If you could half keep up with him, you could catch the rest pretty easily. And we knew he wasn't hurting the resources real bad.

When you get to track someone like the King of the Poachers, you get to know their habits. You know if he passed on some eagle feathers it's because he found a carcass. You know he would never kill a bird of prey—they're like his cousins. You know if he's over his limit on fish it's because he's going away on a construction job and his family needs them while he's away.

You come to appreciate these values even if they don't conform to the rules. You get kind of fond of guys like these. There's almost an intimacy to the relationship. Heck, these guys will often intentionally lead you to the commercial meathunters.

The King could read nature's signs better than us. He operated on instincts, not the rule book or scientific studies. He often knew about a nuisance problem with bear or beaver before we did. And he had the situation cleared up before we responded to the first complaint.

Our King of the Poachers had a sense of humor too. He knew how to pull fast ones on those Illinois weekenders who like to skirt the law. They like to buy venison and they'll pay premium prices for it. But our King ran a scam on them that involved the same pile of hides and old cull cows that he'd buy down in the Fox Valley and then butcher. He made it seem like he was running a big deer meat operation and all he did was supply them with thousands of pounds of old stringy beef.

This cat-and-mouse thing between the elite poacher and the law goes back hundreds of years. Back to the time when the kings claimed all the game and hunting was forbidden to the common people. Yet even then there were skilled poachers who won the grudging admiration of their pursuers.

So we do share this bond. It's the inside-outside thing. You know, there are inside people and outside people. Those who love the outdoors have this bond. And that's how it is with the King of the Poachers.

He looked like one of us. A burly guy, bushy beard, plaid shirt, and calf-high boots. He ate at the same fish fries. He tipped suds at the same taverns.

One time I even shared a sunset with the King of the Poachers. It was totally by accident. I just happened to have my son in the canoe in the Caldron Falls flowage. He was just drifting in his canoe, paddle across his knees. He was doing the same thing we were doing. Just soaking in those crimson and purple reflections off the water.

I realize that it must appear unseemly that a former law enforcement officer would have this respect for someone he should arrest. Especially in these troubled times, you want people to play by the rules. But we need an uncaged soul or two among us to remind us of the old natural freedoms.

The King of the Poachers was that uncaged soul. He was a remnant of the old ways, the old connections to the land.

He disappeared a few years back. Maybe an accident out on a lake. Too bad he never got a funeral. It would have drawn a hundred brush cops.

But you never know. There was never a body. His family moved away. A funny thought occurred to me. What if the King of the Poachers was working undercover for another agency?

Fox River Coureur du Bois

France and French culture made their marks on Wisconsin at an early date. The first hundred years of European exploration of Wisconsin was almost entirely a French enterprise.

Despite the presence of dozens of French surnames throughout Wisconsin, awareness of French heritage does not approach that of Norwegians and Germans. In part, the lower profile is due to dispersal. There are few solidly French areas in Wisconsin. In places like Green Bay, Two Rivers, Marinette, and Prairie du Chien, one can find a presence but not neighborhoods.

The other reason for the fading of French heritage has to do with their pattern of settlement. They were often lone trappers or traders. Only the French Canadian immigrants of the lumber era came in groups with families.

Then too, they were remarkably flexible about national allegiances. Intermarriage with other national groups and races was not taboo to them. Ejection of France from North America, militarily and politically, left individuals to arrange personal alliances with British, Canadian, Spanish, or U.S. military officials.

There are many family heirloom stories about French ancestry. Most tend to emphasize (or invent!) aristocratic roots. It is refreshing when a descendant finds delight in an ancestor outside the pale of society's approval. Let Peter, a De Pere carpenter, tell of his family's connection to that wonderful French American tradition of the frontier rogue.

🌾 🌾 🌾

When I started looking at the family tree I didn't even know what *Coureur du Bois* meant.

We always knew that we had French blood, but there were few French traditions in our family. Not like all the Irish and Polish holidays and rituals.

Of course, I soon found out—I asked the priest—that *Coureur du Bois* means "runner in the woods." But it took more research before I really understood the term. I thought it was a term for *messenger*.

"It turns out that it was a catch-all phrase for a category of renegades, poachers, outlaws, and unlicensed voyageurs—men who lived outside the rigid environment of the forts and Jesuit missions.

My ancestor actually used "Du Bois" as a last name. It's a pretty common French name. But I think that he really came out of the Radisson and St. Clair families who called him "little nephew."

I was mighty impressed to find out what a scoundrel he was. Quite the ladies' man—that still runs in the family, if you don't mind my saying so.

He had children by at least four different women. He had the brothers of some hunting for him and wanting to duel. He supposedly shot the ear off of one defender of virtue. He never legally married before any judge or priest, although with respect to my particular line, the woman in question was part Menominee and the arrangement was blessed by a chief or something.

Most of the stories about my ancestor focus on the Fox River and his dealings with the Indian tribes, mostly about contests. Fishing contests. Canoe contests. Hunting contests. The usual stuff about who was stronger, faster, smarter, and so forth. Supposedly the Indians liked his tricks. They forgave him many slights that from other men would have led to their scalps decorating a lodge pine.

One of the best I heard in that vein was the duck-hunting story. A Menominee man challenged him to see who could bring back the most ducks. Du Bois knew that the Menominee would probably get more ducks, so he had to come up with something that would at least amuse them.

So he came into the Green Bay settlement to think about what he could do. He was in luck. A merchant ship sailed in that day. Among the cargo on the boat just happened to be a big cage of white ducks. He bought them with ten times their value in beaver pelts.

Now the Menominee didn't have much experience with domesticated ducks. Probably never saw white ones. So when Du Bois led a long line of ducks into camp it caused quite a commotion. No one saw him dribbling the corn behind him.

He said, "Behold the master hunter who makes the ducks fall from the sky at his command and bids their ghosts to follow him to the feast!" His Menominee friends were very impressed. At least until he told them that such ghost ducks could be eaten unplucked and uncooked.

His hunting competitors grabbed up some ducks to realize the promise of succulent spirit flesh. Soon ducks were squawking and the hunters were spitting out feathers. Then there were belly laughs all the way around.

This makes some people think that Du Bois was really Radisson. Radisson was big on such jokes. The Iroquois called Radisson by the name "Dodcon," or little devil.

Among the other stories are things about his journeys. Canoeing and portaging down to Prairie du Chien or into Minnesota. Travels with British soldiers or American soldiers—whoever was paying the most.

His other trait that amused people was his running feud with the priests. He actually liked them, but he couldn't resist tormenting them. He'd sour their wine. Cut holes in the rear ends of their cassocks. Put snakes in their beds. Things like that.

Probably his most famous joke is when he tricked the old Green Bay priest into the sweat lodge. He had the old boy real interested in Indian religion. He filled the priest's head with all sorts of made-up mumbo-jumbo. Stuff about spirits and demons. He told the priest that sweat lodge ceremonies produced visions of such things.

So he got the old priest up to a little village on Lake Poygan. Got him stripped down and pushed him into the sweat lodge. He didn't tell the priest that the lodge was filled with naked widows. There were lots of giggles from the women and screams from the priest. I guess the priest got yanked pretty good in there.

My nephew asked me what the point of this old story is. That's hard to answer.

But I told him how I think it has something to do with why our family does some of the things it does. It's why we find pleasure in hunting and the drinking and card playing in the cabin. It's why we tend fires through the night to make maple syrup or put up with the bugs and heat to pick berries.

I asked him if he remembered what it was like the first time he went with the men on the smelt run. When he smiled and said yes, I told him that's his Du Bois part.

Haystack Hilda

Heroic tales and stories of feats of strength are typically a male domain. Female parallels to the Paul Bunyan and John Henry legends are rare.

However, Wisconsin is an excellent place to find these larger-than-life women. Its northern European stock makes for some physically large women, and pioneer hardships have made others large of heart.

A number of such stories can be found on the local level. Osseo boasts a Norwegian Viking maiden story. Douglas County claims a Finnish huntress in the style of the goddess Diana. Dane, Dutch, Swedes, and Scots have similar stories told by families scattered throughout the state.

But it is the German Americans who harbor the most Wisconsin Amazons. Hints of such stories can be found in the rural communities around Sheboygan, Manitowoc, Watertown, and Eau Claire.

The most fleshed-out of these Teutonic tales can be found west of Wausau in the farming country surrounding Marathon City. From there north to the towns of Berlin and Hamburg one can find a belt of nineteenth-century German farms with their large forebay barns.

It was and is an area of sturdy farm women. The men beam with pride about wives with strong backs and ample size. This individual spousal pride is eclipsed by the collective celebration of the "godmother" of all these stocky helpmates: Haystack Hilda.

If you visit the Arrow Tap in Marathon City during the early afternoon, you might find Reinhold, a short elderly gentleman with stories to tell. If there's a break in all the talk about weather, high school football, and ginseng prices, you might ask him about the toughest woman in Wisconsin history.

🌾 🌾 🌾

You betcha she was big and strong!

She was bigger than most men. And lots of muscle too. Hands like a loading-dock worker. They called her Haystack Hilda on account of her profile. If you saw her silhouette on the twilight horizon, you'd swear it was a haystack.

Speaking of haystacks—which of course nobody makes anymore—old Hilda could pitch a whole haystack up on a wagon or up

57

in the haymow with one flick of a hayfork. Making hay for her wasn't any more trouble than raking the leaves.

She was a handsome woman for her size—a pleasant dimpled face, flaxen braided hair, ruddy complexion. She was over six feet tall, by how much I'm not sure, and weighed probably three hundred pounds in her prime, but she lost some muscle and weight in her later years.

She was more muscle than fat. Just broad. Broad back. Broad buxom chest. And a broad backside. She filled a love seat all by herself. And her arms and legs, good God, they were like those of a professional wrestler. She could get a steer in a headlock, and she could crack open a nail keg between her knees.

Now, don't get me wrong, she wasn't a showoff. She started into these feats of strength as a matter of necessity. She was a widow, you see. Widowed three times if I recollect right.

She just had to do that farm work when those men died. She had about ten kids, but they weren't much help until they got older. And after the third husband died, she just found men too undependable.

Some say it all started when her work horse ran away. There was plowing to be done so she slipped the collar and harness over her head and body. Her eight-year-old son guided the plow.

She had to be strong because she had to take care of a farm, a bunch of kids, and sometimes an ailing husband. She was either nursing one or burying one. But that heavy farm work gave way to other things. She started to get a lot of attention for her strength and soon she was able to make money off of it.

First, neighboring farmers called upon her to hold up corners of buildings while they replaced sill logs and foundations. Then she got a reputation for handling angry bulls. She punched them and knocked them out cold.

Next, she was working the county fairs. That started right here in Marathon County. That's when it turned from work to competition. That and money.

Hilda won a weightlifting contest. Then she beat and whipped a bear. Then a boxing kangaroo. She won nice little cash purses on those deals.

So she moved up, taking on traveling prizefighters and wrestlers. She never lost a match. Made enough on some of those fights that she could have retired. But she was a thrifty German and she bought enough land so that she could give each son a farm of his own.

She had other talents besides her strength. She was quite a singer and could shake a barn with her voice. She sang with the old German liederkranz and was often a guest singer when the German operas came to Wausau.

Hilda also could recite the old epic poems and sagas. She knew all about the old German mythic characters. But that was before all the anti-German hysteria in World War One.

Oh, yeah, about those dead husbands. They may have been on the frail side to begin with. And let's face it, men didn't live as long in those days.

But there was always the rumor that it wasn't illness that sent them to early graves. The talk around the area was that she wore them out, if you know what I mean.

To this day it is a sign of utmost danger if a pair of extra-queen-size bloomers are flapping on a washline.

Washington's Last Soldier

Revolutionary War soldiers are common folklore characters in the eastern United States. Only a handful of those original patriots were hardy enough to make the trek to the Wisconsin Territory four and five decades later.

But some did and there are records of their burials in the southern tier of Wisconsin counties. Others of unusual background found their way to Stockbridge and Portage where patriot Mohicans and remnants of other eastern tribes were buried after loyal service as scouts and trackers.

Perhaps as many as three dozen European American and two dozen American Indian patriot veterans lie in forgotten Wisconsin cemeteries. A few British and Tory veterans may also rest here.

Prairie du Chien is a focal point for much frontier lore, and one can find pioneer stories by the dozens in that Crawford County community. Not surprisingly it is also home to a variety of stories involving veterans of the Black Hawk War, the Winnebago Wars, the War of 1812, the Revolutionary War, and at least one veteran of the French and Indian War.

The most colorful of these involves a flamboyant Frenchman. Stephen tells this heirloom tale from his old Prairie du Chien family with much French blood in their veins.

🔥 🔥 🔥

Jean Rivard, my ancestor, was the last of Washington's soldiers.

By that I mean the last one in Wisconsin. He lived almost up to the Civil War. That means he was well over one hundred years old. Unfortunately records cannot establish his exact age.

He thought he was born near present-day Wheeling, West Virginia, of a French trader father and Shawnee mother. He was orphaned at an early age and relocated to Fort Pitt at Pittsburgh. From there he made his way back to the eastern colonies.

As a young man he was caught up in America's War of Independence. When France entered the war on the American side he was a valuable asset as a liaison.

At one time there was a lot of speculation that Rivard served directly with the French troups or with Lafayette. But I have determined that he served under General Mühlenberg, a rather unique individual in his own right. Mühlenberg was a German-speaking, Greek-poetry-reciting Lutheran minister who masterminded the rout of the British at Yorktown.

Since that final victory was coordinated with a French naval blockade, Rivard played an important role in the outcome. But Rivard was a restless sort and the lure of the frontier tugged at him. He went back to the Ohio River country of his birth. And he fell into the companionship of men like him who blazed the trails from the Ohio country to the Rockies.

Many were of mixed French and Indian parentage like himself. But there were also many mixed blood frontiersmen whose surnames identified them as Dutch, Swedish, German, and Scotch Irish.

They were handy men to have around on the frontier, especially during the War of 1812. They helped fight the battles of the Ohio country and Great Lakes. They led the raids into Canada.

Rivard arrived here in the advance party that ultimately knocked the British out of Prairie du Chien, so he was set up comfortably at Fort Crawford for a time, took a Winnebago wife, and tried to be a merchant. He made a profit but had itchy feet.

He ranged the wild country. He knew most of the mountain men, trappers, and scouts of the pre-Mexican War time. He knew Boone and Crockett. He and Boone went out to the Yellowstone country before Lewis and Clark.

He always came back to Prairie du Chien to check on his wife. She ran the business better than he did, so he was well-off. We always say in our family that it was her Winnebago business sense that started our four or five related families on the way to prosperity.

As he got older he roamed less. But young men, military leaders, and adventurers still sought him out. They came to Prairie du Chien to seek his counsel. It is said that Colonel Dodge visited him before and after the Black Hawk War.

One by one he buried his old friends in the Fort Crawford burial grounds. Old Keim from Pennsylvania. Van Patton from New York. Shopteeka the Potawatomi scout. All the old Mohican, Narraganset, Delaware, Ontario, Kickapoo, and Winnebago Indian trackers from the old frontier wars.

When Rivard finally died, the old-timers gave him a big sendoff. A three-day wake, Indian dignitaries, military honors from veterans of a half-dozen wars. And lots of drinking, with toasts to "Washington's Last Soldier!"

Keeper of the Northern Lights

Wisconsin's "east coast" and "northern shores" are rich repositories of Great Lakes maritime lore, especially concerning lighthouses.

Wisconsin is virtually the world capital of fishing stories. They are connected to every brook, creek, river, flowage, pond and lake, and yes, the Great Lakes. All the original tribes and the various European American groups contribute to this lore.

But despite Wisconsin's abundance of ethnic tales, it is hard to find stories about those seafaring Icelanders who came to Wisconsin. So what could be rarer than a story about an old Icelandic lighthouse keeper told by a fifth generation Icelandic American fisherman?

Washington Island off the tip of Door County is home to one of Wisconsin's least populous minorities. Here a fair-haired young man named Jan works the marina and picks up tourists looking to fish Lake Michigan or Green Bay.

If you can find him around the docks at dusk on those lengthy summer days, you might get him to stop fish cleaning to chat a bit. If you are very, very lucky, and if you listen closely to hear his soft voice over the wind-driven lines snapping the masts and the gulls crying for fish guts, you just might hear a story about the old Icelandic lighthouse keeper.

🌱 🌱 🌱

Ya, I learned the old stories from grandfather, right here on Washington Island.

Grandfather was from the founding family here, a descendant of Arni Gudmundsson. We were among the first twenty families that came from Eyrarbakki, Iceland. This was before Icelanders fanned out through the Dakotas and Canada.

They told lots of stories through the long winter nights—that was an Icelander custom. Partly, they told stories because of the rough life of fishing and cutting cordwood—they didn't farm till later. Partly, they were told through homesickness.

Icelanders had all the usual Norse and Viking stories. We knew of Erik the Red, Leif Eriksson, and the old gods, and the longships. But we had a few special Icelander stories that involved the Northern Lights. Fitting because of Iceland's location.

In our family, it was about the keeper of the Northern Lights. Like all good Icelander stories, it involved the old myths, life close to the water, great adventures, and family history.

Family history was always wrapped up in these legends. Almost all Icelander families can trace their history back a thousand years to Norway, Denmark, or the Norse settlements of Ireland. Almost everyone has a royal ancestor. Every family had a woman who was a seer or a man who was a wizard way back on the family tree. Those magicians were usually said to be the source of family stories.

The story centers on Mori Thorfinnsson, a cousin of Gudmundsson. The Thorfinnsson family went back to the explorers who traveled to America a thousand years ago. They were part of *Njála,* the great Icelandic saga.

Mori Thorfinnsson was on such an adventure when his boat was attacked by Iroquois Indians. A merman came up out of the St. Lawrence River and Mori asked for a charm to save his life. The merman promised Mori immortality if he would perform a task once a year. Mori agreed.

It turned out this task was to tend the Northern Lights, a job that previously occupied all the mermen of the northern seas, lakes, and rivers. Now the old Norse thought of the Northern Lights as Odin's Valkyries riding in fiery glory as they carried dead heroes to Valhalla. But by Mori's time, it was generally accepted that the Northern Lights simply marked the path to Valhalla. They were like a harbor light.

Mori performed the task at annual intervals. Each trip north put him in the stew of more adventures. He sailed Hudson Bay with monsters who traveled in iron boats. He built an ark and took a load of buffalo, elk, and moose back to Iceland for a great feast.

Mori traveled across the plains, climbed the Rockies and swam in the Pacific Ocean. He explored the interior of Alaska. The Indians called him "the man who cannot die" and said it was when Mori killed the great white bear that he turned into a shape changer. He could become any animal he wanted.

So he roamed the world. He fought alongside the Vikings. Even came to Washington Island in the days of a big Indian battle. But each year he performed his job of tending the Northern Lights.

Because he was now an expert in such things, he soon set up a series of signal lights that stretched from Lappland to the Aleutians. They included one right here on the island out at Boyer Bluff. They weren't lighthouses yet, just big bonfires on high points.

By the Middle Ages, he was working with the Spanish and Portuguese on building real lighthouses. And when he had a century or so to kill, he would take up lighthouse keeper duties at lonesome spots. It might be in the Canary Islands or the Orkney Islands. Anywhere north of the Equator that would not interfere with his annual job of tending the Northern Lights.

He would even go home to Iceland every so often. And each time he would settle down for a while. Even father a few children. He was a father in thirty different generations in Iceland.

When the Icelander migration of the nineteenth century came, Mori was the ideal man to advise the young emigrants. He told his cousin Gudmundsson about Washington Island. He even told Gudmundsson about the ideal shelter of Detroit Harbor, the view from Boyer Bluff, and the beaver to be trapped in Big Marsh and Little Marsh.

Eventually Mori came over himself and settled among his great-great-great-great-grandchildren on the island. He even helped plan the Potawatomi light out on Rock Island and the Plum Island light.

We lost track of Mori before I was born. Actually during World War Two. Mori was an old warrior you know. He couldn't sit at home.

A Navy man from here said that Mori caused the Northern Lights to flare one time on the North Atlantic run so that they caught a couple of German U-boats on the surface. Another veteran told me that Mori lured a Japanese convoy onto the rocks by a false light at Attu in the Aleutian Islands.

I wouldn't have known what to make of these faraway stories if it weren't for my own experience. My reserve unit was called up during the Persian Gulf War.

I had a chance to do some sightseeing. So I went to take a look at the old stone Phoenician lighthouse on Bahrain. I climbed the stone stairs and what do I see carved in the top ledge—the name *Mori Thorfinnsson!*

The Culdees of Doty Island

Irish American lore is found throughout Wisconsin. Because Irish settlements are not nearly as prominent as those of the Norwegians and Germans, their stories are a bit more difficult to unearth and interpret. A fair number are urban ghost stories. Complementing those are short accounts of meadow leprechauns and fairies in the rural areas where Ryans and Murphys still till the soil.

But despite the colorful legend and lore of Ireland, it is not common to find complete Irish American folktales that mix Old World references with New World local flavor. So it is a rare treat to find a source with a tale that combines European and North American elements. It is rarer still to find a story that can be placed in the category of pre-Columbus voyages.

The story belongs to Irish Americans throughout the Fox Valley area who hail from Murphy Corner in Outagamie County. The setting is Doty Island, an urbanized isle positioned like a bathtub stopper at the north end of Lake Winnebago.

The source is a young man working his way through college by bartending at an Appleton motel and convention complex. The story starts with a waitress's request for eight brandy old fashioneds.

Granddad a   as t   that gave away Wisconsin's tie to the C

He said th   n'   but they drank brandy long before t   mind that most Irish habits were   reactions to them.

s Old Ireland he spoke   thing from the Middle

d through—he was   favorite Celtic tale involve   children about the Culdee   ox River between Menas   t.

N   escribed them as advent   like refugees and missio   s of New England. Just a

Gr   dees came to North Americ   ver a hundred years. Once   was no way he'd hold

ast followers of Druids.   t Ireland settlements. This   shrines.

But they became very devout Christians.   style of early Christians. And they had the in   le of primitive Christians.

This made them a ta   ucture that came to dominate European politics. But becau   r Druid background, they knew how to hide until things blew   r. For example, Irish King Loigaire protected them during the initial Christian phase. Then

[Handwritten note: Here you go Walker. Sorry about some of the missing pages. You won't miss much. Good reading — Ward.]

King Aed in the sixth century drove them out of their settlements and confiscated their lands at the request of the Church.

This is when the Culdees learned to be voyagers. Their fishermen became their leaders. Fitting Christian metaphor, isn't it?

At first, they hid in the western islands. Then they started settlements in Iceland, Greenland, Newfoundland, and down into New England. In New England, they became associated with the Algonquian tribes. They built structures out of large stones in Rhode Island and Massachusetts. And they traveled on long journeys with the Algonquians.

That's how they got to Doty Island. It was their westernmost settlement. There were at least a dozen buildings in this settlement.

Doty Island was not like it is today. Granddad said the channels were different and there was some higher ground that was leveled off to fill the low spots.

The settlement was on that higher ground, as was a stone chapel constructed of unmortared glacial boulders. The ruins lasted all the way to the beginning of this century. Then, the stones were used for foundations on other buildings.

Even after the Culdees were gone, the Indians used the chapel as a big sweat lodge. The area was sacred and was used as a meeting area for disputes between tribes. There was a cemetery for Culdee Indian converts.

The Culdees attempted to do missionary work among the tribes, but they had few converts. Those at Doty Island were from bands weakened by war or disease.

Most of the tribes along the way were friendly. They just didn't take the strict religious stuff too seriously. They were fascinated by the Culdee lifestyle, but only as a curiosity.

The Culdees still knew their Druid magic, so they were able to pull tricks that gave them a lot of leverage. But those who came to visit them on Doty Island did so for entertainment, not spiritual development.

According to Granddad, the first cheese and wine were made on Doty Island. But unless the Culdees brought goats and grapes with them, it is not easy to figure out how these products were made.

Everybody who hears this story wants to know what happened to the Culdees. Almost everybody wants to hear something to the effect that they became the Menominee tribe. But there's not a romantic ending like that.

The truth is more complex and distressing. It was just inevitable that the Culdees would die out. Think about it. These monk-type cultures don't reproduce very well. Children were a rarity among them.

There were some women. But their role is not entirely clear. Some were probably nuns, and a handful of wives did come along.

But their demise was hastened by their own traits. By that I mean their zest for exploration and their Christian mission. Some scouting parties set off for California and Mexico, but they didn't make it across the Plains.

Their sense of mission had to do with peacemaking. The tribes called upon them to mediate. Many times they had to get between the parties on the battlefield. Naturally that was a risky proposition which claimed lives from time to time.

But the main losses came up on the Door County peninsula. There, a large group of Culdees was killed up at the Door of Death.

They were up there trying to stop a conflict between the Menominee and the Winnebago. Both tribes killed some of the Culdees. But the bulk of them died crossing to the islands when a storm sank their boats.

That's when the tribes knew the Culdees had lost their power. That was the end of the Druid magic. That was the end of the first Celtic settlement in Wisconsin.

Plover's Waynabozo

The American Indian legend of the "trickster" is found throughout the Western Hemisphere. Similar figures can be found in African and European folklore.

Wenebojo of the Great Lakes thrives as the most fleshed-out of these sly and sometimes flawed characters. Hundreds of tales cast him in story plots involving humor, pathos, and tragedy. The Ojibwe stories place him in parables about nearly every form of human activity.

Classic stories of the Ojibwe traditionalists in the Lake Superior belt in Wisconsin, Minnesota, Michigan, and Ontario place Wenebojo squarely in the oral history of spiritual practices. But everyday anecdotes of the modern Woodland peoples consign this figure to folklore terrain similar to that occupied by Ole and Lena in Norwegian American stories.

Indeed, my first brush with a trickster story showed a total expropriation by European Americans. Along the lower Wisconsin River, Wenebojo had become Winny Beaujeau, a ghost with both humorous and larcenous sides (see Driftless Spirits: Ghosts of Southwest Wisconsin*).*

Anthropologists will tell you that American Indian people no longer believe in Wenebojo or no longer consider him an active figure moving among them.

At least one La Crosse resident with one quarter Ojibwe ancestry believes otherwise. Leonard is a self-employed businessman with a history degree. Weekend outings are the cover for his ongoing hobby of tracking down forgotten tribal village sites.

One such trip took him to the Plover area to search for signs of ancestors. He found more than he bargained for.

☙ ☙ ☙

We think that the Plover site is the furthest south Chippewa village discovered so far and the only abandoned site with an active story tradition.

Now, you are going to ask how a village abandoned for over a hundred years can have any traditions. To understand that, you need to understand the concept of the southern Chippewa.

That's our background. We were outside the ceded territory and lost official tribal status. These were small bands, often associated with Potawatomi or Ottawa. Sometimes they went south and west to hunt buffalo with their Sac, Fox, Miami, and Illinois cousins.

Over the years, many lost track of their background. Intermarriage and assimilation dulled memories of the old stories.

But around Plover, we found a stubborn little cluster of southern Chippewa where the traditions survived, admittedly with some unique twists. That's where I ran into Joe, the darkest guy with a Norwegian name I have ever met.

He was quick to tell me his Indian Name: Waynabozo. I didn't catch on at first. His pronunciation was different, and my ear for

70

Anishinabe is not the best. Besides, I am a little leery of the Indian name stuff. Some are very lyrical, but nonauthentic. Then, others are just jokes pulled by shady medicine men which translate to things like "whizzing skunk" or "scratches butt.'

But Joe cleared it up real quick for me. He said his family and the old Plover band were *the* Wenebojo descendants. He said the band stayed in central Wisconsin as kind of a rear guard to keep the whites off balance.

He was quick to add—with a totally deadpan delivery, I might add—that the eventual settlement of the area by Poles and Scandinavians left the area handily off balance. So with their main task completed, they settled into generations of relative obscurity.

For a guy who had never done the powwow circuit or sat in a teaching lodge, he was very familiar with his remote ancestor, Wenebojo. He knew the variations in the stories and, in an uneducated way, the sociology of the stories.

He knew Wenebojo as the original man or the half-human transitional figure between us and the spirits. He knew him as a shape-shifter who could turn himself into animals.

Joe was able to place his "grandfather" in the main legends: the creation, the flood, the purification of Earth, and the construction of what we call North America, Turtle Island. He had a crude understanding of how these legends related to sacred practices.

But the legends were distorted through years of separation from tribal life. The sacred circle and passing of the pipe were replaced by campfire sharing of a bottle in a paper bag. The ancient lessons about the environment and survival were transformed into off-hand stories about snowmobile repair and extraction of ice-fishing shacks that had fallen into lakes.

It was Joe's own personal stories that were most faithful to the trickster tradition. Or maybe I should say jokester. Joe's tales of lessons he had learned were closer to the tradition of stand-up comedy than the medicine lodge. His statements were more deserving of a lounge band rimshot than a ceremonial "a-ho."

He would start solemnly about the traditions of hunting. He would express deep feelings about the relationship between the hunter and the whitetail deer. He would allude to the profound lessons to be learned while hunting the whitetail. Then he would sum it up by saying, "The chief lesson of whitetail hunting is that a hunter needs blaze orange toilet paper."

Or he might talk about the sacredness of food. Say stuff about how people need to return to a natural diet. Next thing he's off making disparaging remarks about his wife's love of fry bread, saying, "With her, I call it thigh bread...and butt bread, too."

And he loved to tell stories about lessons he had learned from local white people. He would pose them as questions. Like, "Why did the truck full of potato pickers die when the driver drove them into the Wisconsin River?" The answer, "Because they couldn't get the tailgate open."

You may know that the very old Canadian Anishinabe stories place Wenebojo in the context of his family relationships. He is the youngest of the four sons of Winona and the Manitou of the West. Joe focused on the earthy side of their origins. Joe spoke extensively on the manly physical attributes and endurance of the Manitou.

The social scientists will tell you that Wenebojo is part of tribal lore from the Maritime Provinces to the American Southwest. They say that he was the central figure in the oral histories of hunting cultures and that he was a more marginal character in agrarian tribal groups.

But what of today? Who is he for today's Indian? I can't answer that question for the tribal traditionalists who find their truth in the silent vision fasts in the deep woods of reservations.

For those of us cut off from much of our past and living in isolated pockets, I think he represents the humor we use to get through strange and stressful situations. He is our buffer from the outside world.

So I really believe that Joe from Plover is Waynabozo. He performs that role for his little group. And I believe every urban Indian community center, every bingo hall, every smokeshop, and every group of college students fresh off the reservation has one.

Nels Niklaus of Scandinavia

Christmas lore has undergone significant shifts over time. Celtic and Germanic solstice feasts evolve into Christian holidays. Even through the Christian era, the celebration switches back and forth from pious contemplation to drunken revelry, depending on the century and location.

Social scientists and historians tell us that Christmas was subverted from its religious purpose at a very early stage. They are quick to add that the holiday always had an underlying commercial and social context.

In old Europe, Christmas brought relaxation of trade and travel restrictions. It also provided an opportunity for demonstrations of benevolence on the part of feudal lords. It was a valued respite in the darkest time of year from the stalking specters of war and pestilence.

Christmas customs varied greatly from place to place. Generally, the customs simply absorbed the pre-Christian practices of the area and its people. Feasting, music, and dancing were common forms of celebration except in Puritan and Inquisition times.

Yet, it was storytelling that was the most widely observed Christmas tradition. Storytelling united the time of the Christ Mass with the time of the older pagan rituals. Stories of death and rebirth, seasonal change, and renewed hope out of despair were interwoven in the psychic fabric of northern peoples awaiting spring.

Christmas is perhaps second only to Halloween in the number of stories generated by holiday traditions. But it is clearly first in terms of the broad impact of its central stories revolving around the character known today as Santa Claus.

Be he St. Nicholas or Father Christmas, the Sinta Klaus of northern Europe is an integral component of the popularized secular holiday. In a time of corporate downsizing and get-tough-on-the-poor government policies, he is the only nonjudgmental and generous figure left in American culture. Retailers shamelessly exploit his New Deal sensibilities.

Still, much information about St. Nick has been lost along the way. He was not always the sanitized advertising and greeting card figure that we see today.

Emmett, a retired cabinetmaker in Ogdensburg, has the Wisconsin spin.

When I grew up in Scandinavia, it was Nels Nicklaus we heard about at Christmas. Santa Claus was for city kids, not for good Scandinavians, at least in our little enclave in western Waupaca County.

We didn't have a pure culture by any means. Our family circle was mixed. Mostly Norwegian, but with a sprinkling of Danes, Swedes, Dutch, and one Door County Icelander thrown in for good measure. A lot of Knutsons and Petersons, I recall.

Back in those poor days, the idea that everyone would get a gift—even if they were no good potlickers—was unheard of. It was a time to reward good and to punish bad.

Nels Niklaus performed that function. He was no liberal. He had a rough side to his character. A little bit like an old Norwegian bachelor uncle who had spent too much time in the logging camps.

Nels Niklaus was part saintly figure, part hanging judge. Like a tough country justice of the peace, he sorted out the good kids from the bad kids. The good kids got some oranges and some warm clothes. The bad kids got the limber basswood switch on their rear ends.

Now, I've done a little bit of research on this stuff. I know we weren't the only ones who saw this aspect of St. Nick. Lots of places he had either an evil twin, a tough cookie helper, or just a dark side of himself.

Maybe I should say a dark side or a dim side. Sometimes it was a matter of a lust for vengeance. Other times, it was like he wasn't too bright.

This figure shows up in Germany's Rhine Valley and eastern France as Pelz Nickel, which means "Fur Nicholas." He was quick with the rod on little naughty behinds.

In Holland, the Nicholas was a long-bearded, shaggy figure who made disturbing noises at night. It was almost as if he was haunting evil doers.

In England, he made the rounds of the homes of the wealthy and demanded booty from them. He had a touch of a shakedown artist to him, or maybe a protection racketeer.

One thing's sure, he was no billboard Santa with a suit fresh back from the dry cleaners. No, he was more like a homeless guy you'd see sleeping on a heating grate down in Madison. Hair and beard untrimmed. A little bit of breakfast egg still hanging in the beard. A bit smelly—bathing wasn't an obsession back then.

He was tricky and shifty. Like a railyard hobo. You couldn't let a pie cool on an open windowsill if he was around. Or let a new pair of longjohns dry on the line.

This trick part might mean he was part Indian. I heard they have a character who's part magician, part holy man. Supposedly, he can even appear in different ways so you can't recognize him from one time to the next.

But the only bit of evidence I ever heard linking Niklaus to the Indian trickster was the story of how to thaw him out after frostbite. If Nels Niklaus showed up at your house with ice in his beard and that sleepy hypothermia look, you were supposed to melt a cup of lard and make him drink it. Grandpop said two shots of brandy in the mug was a good idea too.

Now, with the Indians, there's a similar story. Among the Chippewa, there were people who were turned into ice creatures through magic. The only way to get them back to normal was to have them drink melted bear tallow. Who knows, maybe the Norwegians and the Indians both got this angle from the Eskimos.

But I don't want you to get the idea that Nels Niklaus was just a bum or a troublemaker. There was that fairness side to him. Not just the dispensing of justice in the form of goodies and lickings, but a basic recognition of how things are and how they should be.

He understood the idea of social class that gets covered up in America. He knew that not everyone is in the same situation. And he grasped that not everyone in a bad spot was morally defective and that not everyone well-off had gotten there honestly or through their own effort.

I know I told you he was not a liberal, but he was a progressive. Even as kids, we understood he had an agenda. I recall that he showed up one Christmas with a Phil La Follette button on the lapel of his raggy coat.

He made us feel good with the little parables he told us. Meek inherit the Earth, no rich men in Heaven stuff. You might say it made us feel good to know he wouldn't visit the banker who foreclosed on the neighbor's farm.

No oranges and handmade wool mittens would go to that rich house. No special maple sugar candy or warm cider. Sure, the kids in that big house might get a shiny new train. But it wasn't from Niklaus. It was a train paid for by the tears of raw-boned farm wives and the grumbling bellies of hungry children.

Some say that Nels Niklaus was just our heavy drinking Uncle Sven dressed up like a fat scarecrow. Maybe in my time that was true. But the story was older than that. Grandpop believed in Nels Niklaus and that's good enough for me!

The Welsh Prince

Many northern European groups have stories of pre-Columbus exploration of North America. Old manuscripts tend to bolster most of these claims.

In Wisconsin, these legends are heavily weighted toward the old Norse legends. Most of these stories are imbued with regional ethnic flavor.

However, there are a number of non-Norse stories that enliven folklore. The German, Poles, English, Scots, and Irish have variations on these stories in many of their old settlements. Of these, only the Irish American tales parallel stories in the Old Country.

This Welsh variation, like the Irish stories, also harkens to European roots. But it differs in two important respects: It is found in only one Wisconsin location, and it is the subject of bitter controversy in Wales itself.

Mineral Point is home to this rare find. Lloyd, a local antique dealer of Welsh ancestry, brims with pride at the telling of the tale.

He warms up his audience with a round of drinks at the bar of the Royal Inn.

🔥 🔥 🔥

If you're not Welsh, you're something else.

I believe the Welsh Prince discovered America before Columbus. And before the Vikings and those lost Irish.

It's true that much of the story is lost in the mists of history. Historians argue about the details. They argue about names and places and dates.

Then there's much argument about how far the Welsh Prince made it into America. Whether he just landed on the East Coast or whether he crossed the continent hundreds of years before Lewis and Clark.

In Wales, some call him Prince Madoc. Supposedly the son of King Owain Gwynedd of Wales. Part of the problem is that the records of that time mention other sons but not Madoc. Madoc's name only shows up in later poems and songs.

One of the trips was around the year 1170. But I think there was one before that and several after that.

It is thought that three of the four expeditions were absorbed into Indian tribes. One group became a band called the "Doegs." They were affiliated with the Virginia Tuscaroras and the Maryland Susquehannocks. Those groups, in turn, were absorbed into the Iroquois Confederacy. I should point out that the old Welsh councils resembled the Iroquois political organization.

One of the other groups became part of the Mandan tribe. That shows you how far west the Welsh made it. It probably means that they did get to the Pacific Ocean.

The Welsh influence with the Mandans was very strong. They had a lot of rosy complexions and even quite a few blue eyes. But the real evidence was in the Welsh-like words in the Mandan language.

The other group that went Indian was right here in Wisconsin. It was the Kickapoo tribe when they lived in the area from Viroqua down to Rock Island. That was in the days long before the Sauk moved into that territory.

The Welsh Prince came right through this area. Out of Illinois, through Green County, over to Darlington, up to Mineral Point, and across to Richland Center. That's where the Kickapoo had their big village.

The Welsh Prince joined the Kickapoo in battle against the Winnebago and the Sioux. There was a great battle fought at Prairie du Chien in this war. Out of this conflict came stories about the Welsh warriors. There was also a story about a Chief Maddock.

Was it Prince Madoc? Or was this the result of a Kickapoo-Welsh marriage? It's hard to know how much Welsh blood stayed with the Kickapoo. But the influence stayed a long time. Welsh was still spoken in the Kickapoo Valley when the French came down the Wisconsin in the 1600s.

This connection later proved valuable to the British Empire. It was these Welsh-Kickapoos who were key to helping to organize Indians against the Americans. They worked that angle through Tecumseh's efforts, Pontiac's Uprising, and the War of 1812. They were incredible warriors.

But as you know, things did not turn out that well for them. Wars took a toll. Other tribes pressed west. The Winnebago got the upper hand. The final blow came when they sided with Black Hawk. They became homeless and nomadic.

That was the Welsh in them. The Kickapoo remnants traveled all over the country. To the Pacific Northwest and to the desert Southwest.

The last piece of this puzzle that I could track was right here in Mineral Point. In the 1890s an exhibition show—sort of like a wild west carnival—came through town. An old Kickapoo was in the show. They called him the Welsh chief. He told quite a few stories as part of the show.

My grandfather remembered many of the stories. The Battle of Prairie du Chien. The adventures up through Lake Superior and the Boundary Waters. But the story that stuck with our family was about the Welsh Prince.

The Welsh chief kept the story alive for eight hundred years and brought it full circle to Mineral Point. So you're treading on ground that is genuinely Welsh.

Remember, if you're not Welsh, you're something else!

Ole Bolle

Paul Bunyan has eclipsed most of the older stories about heroes of the pine-logging era. Many local legends of woodsmen have failed to offer the color and wild hyperbole of the giant man with the blue ox.

Yet, many of these more parochial tales offered a far more realistic view of the work and community aspects of the big timber era. Their heroes were far more accessible and human. Their narrators were far more likely to draw upon experience and family ties to flesh out the stories.

In Wisconsin, almost all the various ethnic groups contributed heavily to logging lore. Northern Europeans were the main contributors. American Indian contributions, mainly from the Bad River Ojibwe and the Menominee, also placed an indelible stamp on timber legends.

But of all the groups, Norwegian Americans have the deepest psychological tie to logging stories. Dozens upon dozens of elderly Norwegian Americans can spin yarns of ancestors' exploits in the big woods. They talk of courage, strength, adventure, and humor.

In the folklore realm, the Norwegian imprint is visible from the opening of the folksong ditty ("My name is Yon Yonson/I come from Visconsin/I vork as a lumberjack der") to the fictional logging tools that draw stares and laughs at roadside attractions.

Have a slice of pie at the Norske Nook in Osseo and hear Emory's claim about the granddaddy of all Norwegian American logging stories. The silver-haired gentleman relays the story from his grandfather.

🌿 🌿 🌿

Grandpop knew Ole Bolle personally. They met each other in the lumber camps. They worked the Black River, the Chippewa River, and up to Lake Superior. Them and a thousand other Norwegians.

Norwegians were the backbone of the logging business, and you might say that Ole Bolle was the iron rod in that backbone. He was as tough as they come, yet gentle with children and filled with belly laughs.

You needed all those qualities to get through life in the woods. You needed to be all that when you were working your behind off one minute and crushed dead by a log the next. In the prime logging days, they said a Norwegian a day was killed in the woods.

Ole Bolle was fearless. He laughed off the smashed finger, broken toes, and axe cuts to the legs. He came from a long line of stubborn Norwegians from way back.

That's the stock the best loggers came out of. Norwegian woodsmen, Arctic fishermen, clipper sailors, and ham-fisted blacksmiths were the ancestors of our loggers. Ole Bolle was the orphan of a merchant seaman.

Bolle was short for Bollerud. And Ole was just a standard Norwegian nickname. I think his real given name was Severt. But he was called Willy, Gus, and Red in different camps.

Ole Bolle came to represent the lives of all those young men who crossed the ocean to seek their fortunes. They came from poor families. They had to work hard in the hopes of one day having enough to buy a farm and send back to Norway for a wife.

Ole and the others were just migrant workers, if you think about it. They were all bachelors in the beginning, young fellows looking for an honest dollar and adventure.

It was partly a runaway thing. Ole said that Norway was a dour place in those days. A young man with energy couldn't make a move in the Old Country without parents, pastors, and government authorities clamping down on him.

Ole said that was part of the need to be rowdy in the logging camps. It was a break with the Old World and a need to live a life as big as the spaces in the New World.

That bigness came in the stories. Ole laughed at the stories told about him. One of his favorites was about how he brushed his teeth with a forty-foot jack pine and then rinsed out his mouth with a passing waterspout. Another one he liked was about how he planted trees by putting a bundle of saplings in his mouth and spitting them out like bullets.

Then there were the ones about how Ole Bolle always got the upper hand on the Devil. That always mystified real lumberjacks since it was well known that the Devil steers clear of any place real work is going on. But it was said Ole tricked the Devil into thinking a furnace was a sauna.

I guess Ole built a big oak fire in that furnace and bragged it up about it being his new sauna. The Devil came by to see it and Ole offered him the first try. People say that the Devil begged to go back to Hell to cool off.

Then there are the tools that Ole invented. There's the motorless chain saw—a logging chain connected to a saw handle. There was the four-man crosscut saw—which is two regular crosscut saws criss-crossed and welded at the juncture. There's even the skyhook—that item you hang on clouds and use to winch out really big logs.

Ole Bolle brought all the major Norwegian celebrations to Wisconsin. He was the one who started the bonfires on St. Olaf's Day on July twenty-ninth. He made sure Syttende Mai had all the flags, music, parades, and gun salutes. He got the Sons of Norway lodges up and running.

All these celebrations were an excuse to pursue his favorite sport of drinking. He was very fond of homemade moonshine and could drink it by the barrel.

Finally, there's that baloney about Ole being on the dim side. That's just more of the usual slander against Norwegians. Just because he used gunpowder for smoking tobacco in his two-gallon pipe.

And there's that misunderstanding about his use of axle grease as a laxative. You have to understand that a big man with a big appetite would get plugged up by that logging camp food. But it absolutely is not true that he passed wagon wheels and boulders when that grease worked its magic! Maybe a couple of bear skulls and a tree stump or two.

Once he was loosened up, well, everything he did was on a big scale. He said his relief created those hills over toward Neillsville. But he said it with a smile, so what are we to think?

I for one think that those old Norwegian lumberjacks lived the life of giants. They needed giant stories. Ole Bolle just happened to fill those giant tracks in the woods.

Apple Jack

Autumn trips to southwest Wisconsin bring the opportunity to sample crisp apples and tangy cider. Commercial orchards and family roadside operations are scattered throughout the area. But it is Crawford County, especially Gays Mills, that boasts the largest concentration of orchards.

There is no shortage of apple experts in Gays Mills. There, wherever people gather, one can find information on apple growing. Lively arguments flow from discussions about the best apple variety for cider. Nostalgic accounts of hillside orchards are woven into the fabric of many stories relating to springtime, harvest, autumn and Halloween.

It would be a relatively simple matter to assemble an entire book-length collection of stories relating to apple picking, cider pressing, apple butter cooking, applesauce canning, and even spicier stories of distilling apple spirits. There is enough technique in apple growing and diversity in apple varieties to merit a Fox-fire-type compilation of orchard folkways.

Apple-related folklore characters are harder to find. It is almost as if the Johnny Apple-seed story closed off further discussion.

83

Nathaniel, the source of the next story, resents this situation. The resentment flows in part from his view that many other apple pioneers are not given their due. But he also harbors a grudge against Johnny Appleseed that befits his five decades of hard work versus the Romanticism of Ohio Valley folklore.

I first met Nathaniel in Gays Mills in the late 1980s when I was doing the field work for Kickapoo Tales: Folklore in Crawford County. *He was a walking storehouse of apple knowledge. He threw in the story about Apple Jack almost as an afterthought.*

It is natural to assume that tall-tale sources identify closely with their stories. They blur the lines between fantasy and reality. Sometimes it seems as if the story characters are alter egos of the storytellers who serve the purpose of heroic role models.

That impression was stronger in this case than any other circumstance I encountered in preparing this collection.

Come in out of the Indian Summer sun and into the coolness of an orchard packinghouse. Smell the aroma of fresh-picked apples, cider press leavings, and the approach of autumn. See if you can sniff the story behind the story.

🌿 🌿 🌿

Johnny Appleseed has no more to do with real orchard work than a pile of horse apples covered with flies!

This being unfair to the horse apples. At least horse apples make good fertilizer and nourish the tree over time, which is more than you can say for that glorified hobo who traveled around scattering seeds.

Did you ever ask yourself what Johnny Appleseed really did? Well, I'll tell you. The fool spread a lot of lousy crab apples across a dozen states. He spread four or five different apple diseases throughout the Midwest. He didn't develop a single decent variety. He did nothing to improve the species or to contribute to better cultivation.

As far as I'm concerned, he was an upstart. Eccentric at best, maybe a nutcase at worst. Just a crazy derelict with a bag of apple seeds and a cooking pot on his head. No wonder the Indians thought he was a madman!

Hell, we had the real giant of the apple business right here in the Kickapoo Valley. Yeah, we had Apple Jack. He was as Wisconsin as cheddar on apple pie washed down with a Huber beer.

Apple Jack got his size from his dad. They both ran close to seven foot tall. He was the Paul Bunyan of the apple world. He could shake all the apples off a tree with one snap of the wrist. Or he could bend a thirty-foot treetop down in a loop and pick the apples off the peak as gentle as a lamb.

Hands! Holy balls, what hands! He could palm about a dozen fair-sized apples in each hand. With long calloused fingers he could run down a branch like a rake, pull off huge quantities. I often saw him put the rim of a bushel basket between his teeth, reach overhead with both hands, and rake down a full basket with one motion.

That's what made him the top picker. Nobody else ever came close. Nobody ever will. He had tremendous strength, speed, and endurance. I was a bit like that myself as a young man. Men like that do more work before noon than Johnny Appleseed did in a lifetime.

He outpicked the three top Gays Mills pickers of his day added together. Didn't even work up a sweat! A solid picker was thought of as someone who could pick one hundred bushels a day. A topnotch fellow might go over two hundred bushels a day and maybe push three hundred. Apple Jack routinely hit five hundred bushels and sometimes pushed a thousand.

His volume was all the more amazing when you consider his meal breaks. What meals! In the morning, he'd eat a dozen hard-boiled eggs like they were little candies. At lunch he could put away a sandwich that was a whole loaf of bread cut lengthwise with a three-pound beef roast slapped in and topped with a pint of horseradish. Supper was a roasted chicken and a whole pie, apple of course. And he washed it all down with cider by the gallon.

He was quite a sight too! He worked barefoot most of the time. Wore boots only after the first hard frost. Always wore red or blue shirts patterned like bandannas. Always long-sleeved shirts buttoned at the wrist, even on the hottest day. Those old-timers knew that sunlight was not good for your skin day after day.

That might have been the reason for his hair. He wore it like Buffalo Bill or General Custer. Curls down to the shoulder. His was an almost orange-red color as a young man and turned to gray-flecked rust as he aged. It was topped off with a short-brimmed black hat that stayed on his head even while skinny-dipping in the Kickapoo.

Yeah, he was quite a character. Got his name on account of his nipping at the apple liquor jug. He loved to celebrate. All those old-time orchard workers did. Apple Jack never missed a hoedown, barn dance, wedding reception, or church social.

85

He loved to dance. He'd grab one gal after another and wear them out. They use to say that most babies were born nine months after a barn dance. But that wasn't true if Apple Jack was dancing. Those gals was just too tired for anything else. I did pretty good with the ladies too.

He was fond of singing, yodeling, and playing music. His singing was kind of on the growly side, but his yodeling wasn't half bad. He taught himself fiddling and made his own horsehair bow and apple-wood fiddle. I fiddled with him a few times.

And drink! Good God, he was a legend! Down in Prairie du Chien he drank more than fifty men into unconsciousness. It was on a bet. We used to do things like that. He said he could outdrink the bunch and still pick a hundred bushels of apples. He lost the bet, though. He was so soused that he climbed some big white pines and picked a hundred bushels of pine cones.

He was top picker from the time he was twelve until he was eighty-three. And he was in pretty tough competition around here. He would have been champ even longer if he hadn't gone away.

Here's what happened. He was bringing a load of apples down to a Lynxville cider press. The wagon tongue broke and the darn Clydesdale team—they're a flighty breed—ran off.

Those are steep roads coming off the bluff. Apple Jack and that load of cider apples came down like a rocket. The wagon and him hit the ramp at the old feedmill and it just launched them. It was late in the day and people in Lynxville said that Apple Jack rode that wagon right into a blood red sun.

They never found the wagon or a body. Just lots of apples in the river. Hell, people in Thompson Center over in Iowa said a wagon flew overhead and rained down apples.

So what happened to him? Well, there's lots of theories on that. Some say that Apple Jack landed on the moon. But I think he came down in Washington State and started the apple business out there.

Fritz Kleinnagel

Wisconsin's beer-drinking stories are as numerous as the taverns between Kenosha and Superior. They cover the full range of ethnic and regional variations available in the Badger State.

Next to the ghost story, the beer-drinking story is the most durable form of folktale in Wisconsin. In Lafayette County, you can find some that date back to trading posts in the days of the Wisconsin Territory. In La Crosse, every Friday night creates a fresh batch.

The aura of Wisconsin chauvinism surrounding beer drinking gives one pause in selecting a representative story. Many would insist that such a story must originate in Milwaukee. Others would assert that the Northwoods taverns have a superior claim.

A growing sense of social responsibility among drinkers and tavern owners justifies avoidance of the numerous stories involving hapless alcoholics or irresponsible operation of motor vehicles. But it would be pure revisionism to suggest that beer-drinking stories are free of evidence of family pain and encounters with law enforcement officers.

The graying of the beer-drinking populace has lowered consumption while emphasizing the quality represented by the microbrews. There is some evidence that these trends have also improved the caliber of beer-drinking stories.

That is the hope of Gus, a collector of beer memorabilia in Manitowoc. Join us in a basement bursting with glasses, steins, trays, mirrors, signs, bottles, cans, and tavern and brewery fixtures. Cheers!

🌿 🌿 🌿

I'm partial to brewery worker stories. I worked at the old Bleser Brewery here in Manitowoc before I was drafted into World War Two, and I worked for Kingsbury until the 1963 merger with Heileman. The old craft brewers at Blatz in Milwaukee and at Rhinelander had some great stories.

Then there are the bartender stories. Those fellows have seen it all. Some of the best stories come from blue-collar bars near those big assembly plants like Allis Chalmers.

But I think the stories with the most popular appeal are the ones right after the repeal of Prohibition. The best one of those to come to my attention was about Fritz Kleinnagel. He was the champion beer drinker of the Lake Michigan shore—Kenosha up to Two Rivers.

Fritz symbolizes a lot of important things to Wisconsin. With Prohibition ending, you have relief from a silly failed social experiment. The Depression is on and people are in need of a breather from all that high-horse moralism.

Fritz is the real Wisconsin let out of the closet. He's a German American who is an American World War One veteran and no longer has to prove he's loyal. Roosevelt is President, and suddenly being a solid social-democrat and progressive is acceptable again.

You've heard the stories about the hard-drinking and hard-fighting pioneers. Fritz is not like that. What Fritz is about is enjoying life's pleasures, especially beer.

You've heard the drinking contest stories. Stories of gluttony and competitors losing consciousness. Fritz is not like that either. He is more in the great tradition of the trencherman, celebrating the sensual pleasure of food and drink.

Fritz was a man of huge girth and huge beer-drinking capacity. When people talk about the incredible amounts of beer he drank, they do it in reverent tones. He never showed the effect of the alcohol.

He simply became more jolly, more talkative. He told stories—drinking stories and Old Country tales. He danced to the umpah and polka bands. He sang the old liederkranz songs.

But most of all he talked about beer as he drank. He talked about the qualities of the finer beers. He talked about all the old Wisconsin breweries. He told the younger people about the beer drinking at the Turner clubs and the Sunday baseball games.

Fritz didn't brag about it, but he was acknowledged as the most accomplished beer drinker in the greatest beer-drinking belt in the world—from the Illinois line to Green Bay. The fools that tried to keep up were either carried out or left face down in their own slop. Fritz never figured out what the big deal was.

He came from a solid beer-drinking background. He was from the rural Manitowoc Germans, at least on his mother's side with the Hershaus, Grimms, and Kellners. That's out in the towns of Kossuth and Maple Grove. So it was in his genes.

And he came out of the right line of work. You can't be a brain surgeon or an air traffic controller and be much of a beer drinker. You need one of those talking, people-dealing jobs. Sales work produces a lot of them. But some of the best are livestock buyers.

That was Fritz. He was a hog and cattle buyer, so he had occasion to know every county tavern, small town bar, and rural supper club in his territory east of Highway 51.

That's what really goes into being a beer drinker's beer drinker. To know the lay of the land as far as what taverns offer. To know how to handle oneself. And to share this knowledge willingly with others. That's what made Fritz great.

He was a beer drinker's oracle, Olympic gold medalist, and referee rolled into one. He could dispense advice and answer questions. Best place for a beer in Kaukauna, he'd tell you. Rough bars to avoid in Marquette County, he knew. Would the new supper club owners in Watertown make it? His prediction was always on the money.

When Fritz said the best bock beer of the spring was Leinie's this year, Huber the next, and Point the year after, no one argued. It was taken as gospel. If he said the best tavern in Antigo was so-and-so's, that would boost their business for years.

But he also dispensed critical survival advice. He knew where soapy glasses would give you the runs. He knew where bartenders would look out for tipsy drivers and where small town cops would set up speed traps. He could tell where you might be hustled at pool, cheated at cards, and given a social disease.

He lived out a philosophy in which beer drinkers were the ultimate fraternal order. He espoused a platform of beer drinking as a civil right to be defended from all the narrow-minded and tight-assed snoops who live in constant agitation over the lurking fear that someone, somewhere, is enjoying himself.

Fritz was a champion because he embodied the gentleman's beer-drinking code: always help out a lady who's had too much to drink, always help a first-time drinker through the rough spots, and always assist a tavern proprietor in maintaining cleanliness and order. He proclaimed a beer drinker's golden rule: Do no harm and have a good time.

Benton's Soldier Girl

Wisconsin's Civil War heritage is impressive considering its relatively small population in the 1860s. Its newness as a state and its distance from the battlefronts also give retrospective pause in evaluating this heritage.

Those times cannot be evaluated solely in terms of military affairs. Significant social movements left their marks. Political, ethnic, and cultural impacts carried over well into the twentieth century.

Unfortunately, not much is known about the contributions of Wisconsin women to the Union cause. Most of the historical information relating to women focuses on relief organizations and care of the wounded. This invisibility extends to the Wisconsin Civil War folklore. The security of our "homefront" rules out Border State-style stories of women spies and romantic trysts with the enemy.

However, almost every American war has generated both legends and documented cases about women who disguised themselves as soldiers and served alongside their brothers or husbands. Evidence of such a tale popped up in my research of secret societies in Lafayette County.

Old Lafayette County families were divided into secret societies which were either pro-Union or pro-Confederate. Many old families nurtured century-old tales of women passionate in defense of their families' perspectives.

Here, a shy source offers up documentation for a passion and a commitment that goes past political advocacy. Hannah unties the ribbon on a bundle of yellowed letters and beams as she lets the story unfold.

🌿 🌿 🌿

These letters were handed down from mother to daughter for four generations. This is a long line of women whose biggest adventures were keeping order at Four-H meetings or judging jam at the county fair. All sturdy pioneer women from old Benton families, but families where the men got all the attention.

I don't want to turn this into a men versus women thing. Our world's poisoned enough by that already. But I'm disappointed, well, a little angry too, that women have to hide their strengths and their achievements.

Mother said that this sort of thing has been going on a long time. She said there were always women who cured their sick children but kept quiet and let doctors take credit. There were women who reconciled feuding relatives and attributed it to a pastor's intervention. There were mothers who saved their children from harsh and incompetent teachers through unheralded tutoring.

In this case, my great-grandmother's early life was dedicated to the sacred cause of saving the nation during the Civil War. She was just a girl when she participated in the most bloody period in our history.

We know nothing of those circumstances from her own hand or mouth. It is these old letters between her daughters—and their references to an aunt's diary—that reveal the evidence of these extraordinary girlhood experiences.

Her daughters just couldn't get over the hardships and rough treatment a girl in this situation must have endured. They did quite a bit of detective work that deepened their amazement. They used courthouse records in Darlington and muster roles maintained by the Grand Army of the Republic.

Their suspicion was fueled by the many entries for James or Jimmy Zipping in Lafayette County companies. Jimmy was our ancestor's brother and barely ten years old when the war ended. So apparently Great-grandmother assumed his name for enlistment purposes.

They also placed great stock in their aunt's diary entry about a photograph displayed at a Grand Army of the Republic encampment. The picture was of Darlington Company I of the Sixteenth Wisconsin Infantry. The aunt made specific mention of a youthful image in the photograph which despite the shorn hair and coarse cloak, was a ringer for Great-grandmother.

"But their discoveries reached an absolutely gleeful pitch when Grandmother discovered an old document that noted the commendation and promotion of one Jimmy Zipping. Let me read parts of the document recorded in the letter:

> Corporal Zipping's service in the command is seen by his brethren in arms as that of the highest order of distinction.

Campaigns in this service include those concluded at Shiloh, Corinth, Vicksburg, Brush Mountain, Turner's Ferry, Bold Hill, and Savannah, and numerous auxiliary actions and movements in connection thereto.

Said campaigns received note regarding extreme casualties resulting from enemy action and disease.

Corporal Zipping twice received notice, at Corinth and Bold Hill, for retrieval of fallen colors in manner essential to the restoration of order and discipline pursuant to advance upon enemy fortifications under intense fire.

Cessation of hostilities alone inhibit the otherwise unavoidable advancement of Corporal Zipping to the commissioned ranks.

The annals of war offer few parallels of fair youth with depth of comradely devotion so profound.

It is signed by the adjutant of the Sixteenth Wisconsin. It spurred the belief by Grandmother and her sister that their mother and Jimmy Zipping were of one mind, body, and soul.

But it was their final piece in the puzzle that gave them the smug certainty that they sought. These letters record an accidental discovery of a quartermaster receipt signed by Jimmy Zipping. Grandmother's excellent penmanship can be seen to absolutely quiver in excitement with the finding that the handwriting is their mother's!

Their letters in later years drop this triumphant tone. The daughters of this unusual woman came to understand that the Civil War was not a romantic journey. Their illusions of their mother as Joan of Arc gave way to an appreciation of her difficult life.

They came to understand the hardships, horror, deprivations, and male coarseness that must have almost overcome a tender girl. They wondered how those circumstances of physical stress, disease, and danger might have contributed to their's mother's early death.

Please excuse my tears. It is an emotional thing to think about. The strength of these pioneer women. We're all very spoiled now. I look at these letters and put my own little annoyances in their proper place.

There's still an unsolved mystery in all of this. Think about what motivates such great sacrifice. I can only think that it would be love. It would be a privilege to know who or what Great-grandmother loved that much.

Big Boris of Cornucopia

P*aul Bunyan is a national archetype for the widely dispersed characters of the "heroic woodsman" and the "giant lumberjack." Such characters are found in nearly every section of the United States except the desert Southwest and the Great Plains.*

Most of these tales have a clear ethnic slant that serves to emphasize the stereotype virtues and flaws of the various groups. There are dozens of such tales on just Wisconsin Norwegians.

The Germans, Swedes, Danes, Bohemians, Poles, Belgians, and old New England Yankees each have several Wisconsin woodsman stories. Even most of the Wisconsin American Indian tribes (with the possible exception of the Oneida, whose main woodsman story seems to have a New York State setting) have representative stories.

Big Boris appears to be Wisconsin's only Russian woodsman. Indeed, it appears to be one of the very few rural Russian American folktales in Wisconsin.

Ethel, behind the counter at Cornucopia's little store, tells the story short and sweet.

My grandfather told this story about his logging days.

Big Boris, Big Boris. That's how he thought of everything from the old days. Big Boris logging out the Cranberry River country by himself. Big Boris rafting logs across Chequamegon Bay.

We were a small Russian community, maybe a dozen or so families, with just a visiting priest for the Orthodox Church.

Big Boris was the founder of the Siskiwit Bay settlement. That was what it was called before it was Cornucopia. He brought a gang in here to log the tracts between Red Cliff and the Brule River.

The logging arrived late here, after 1900. The peak was 1911 to 1915. Grandfather said the last big tract was Lenawee Creek about 1925.

It was never a big logging crew, but with Big Boris, they set records. Grandfather said the Norwegians and Finns needed three times as many men to produce the same number of saw logs.

Of course Big Boris was a large man. Very close to seven feet. Very broad in the chest. Perhaps sixty-inch chest measurement. Very large arms and legs.

The lumberjacks often competed in chopping down trees with a double-bit axe, and it was said that Big Boris used a common trick to win. If he thought the other contestant was catching up, he'd just butt his belly into the trunk and knock the tree down.

Big Boris learned that trick from Paul Bunyan. Mr. Bunyan, of course, did it a bit differently. Bunyan would just make one cut and then stamp his foot to bring the tree down. Or so said Grandfather.

Here in Corny, the Big Boris stories had him beating all the Finnish, Norwegian, and German lumberjacks. The stories had him defeating them with strength, guile, and humor. He would often distract them, dull their axes, or tie down their saws. He'd hitch their pants to passing horse teams and leave them standing in their longjohns. Or he'd get them drunk ahead of time. Or beat them in eating contests. He was a real champion at the table.

The eating contests here involved the old-time triple cross bread. They were big round rye loaves with three crosses imprinted on the top. Each loaf was served with a foot of sausage and a jar of horseradish. Big Boris had no trouble downing a dozen loaves. No one else ever made it past four or five.

Perhaps the thing that set him off most from the other woodsmen was his way with animals. The other lumberjacks were often hunters or trappers. Big Boris was gentle with animals.

Grandfather said that Big Boris would often get in the harness himself if he saw that the horses or oxen were tired. The lumber camp dogs always gathered round him.

But it was with wild animals that he had the real touch. He tamed wolves and bobcats. He played with bears. He would often take whole families of bears swimming right here in Corny. He was one of those hairy men so you could not tell him from the bears at a distance, except that he was bigger.

He often fished the run on the Brule with the bears. He swatted trout out of the water with his big hands just like bears do.

He was last seen in the early 1920s. The government tried to send some Russians home about that time. Big Boris swam out to the Apostle Islands with the bears. Some say he lived out there the rest of his life. But the Canadian Russians say he went up there.

Who knows?

Shawano's Geek

Unsavory and unattractive characters find their niche in folklore. They range from desperadoes to the deformed. Almost every form of personality disorder and disfigurement is celebrated in some subculture.

The "freak show" as it functioned as a carnival and circus mainstay was an unabashed celebration of some of the most flamboyant of these traits. It had a century-long run in America's culture and dimmed finally because of a combination of political correctness and even more shocking entertainment.

Wisconsin's place in circus history provides us with a treasure trove of freak show stories. From Merrill to Baraboo, we are blessed

with many anecdotes about fat men, bearded ladies, sword swallow-
ers, contortionists, fire eaters, and so forth. Occasionally, a freak show
character even rises, like the Scotch Giant, to a folklore persona outside of circus lore.

Of all the bizarre and revolting characters within this milieu, the
Geek was perhaps the most disturbing and affirming to freak show
attenders. Even the most deprived homesteader who had traveled to
a nearby rough and tumble town to see a circus could feel culturally
superior to the Geek.

The shock value of the Geek resided in his total ignorance of
morality, manners, and moderation. This prince of the repugnant
observed no civilized boundaries.

Many people supposed that the circus geeks were aboriginal
people from exotic lands. Stories of kidnapping and virtual slav-
ery were common. The carnival barkers often spun tales about
hidden tribes in Africa, lost valleys in Borneo, or newly discovered
tropical islands.

Step into a Shawano coffee shop where Ed cooks and smell the java
and the cigarette smoke. Sniff out the story of one such "wild man!"

🌿　🌿　🌿

I call him the Shawano Geek because he was originally from
Shawano.

He wasn't billed that way in the circus. It's just the name we had
for him in our family stories. He was a distant relative, you know. It's
not something we were proud of, being the Geek family. Not something where Shawano would put up a sign declaring itself the home
of the Geek.

There's more to the family side of the story too. There was always
the hint of incest here too. By my generation, it was kind of covered
up, so we don't know if it was cousin with cousin or something worse.
But that was at the core of the story.

They thought the inbreeding is what made him a Geek. They didn't
know what was wrong with him exactly. It's not like they had testing
for that stuff in those days. So we don't know if he was retarded or
mentally ill. But it doesn't hurt to talk about it now since everybody
who was embarrassed by it is dead.

Our Shawano Geek went under many different names in many
different shows. But the stories were usually the same. Either he was

supposed to be from some primitive race or he was supposed to have been raised by apes or wolves.

The routine was pretty standard. He ate a lot of raw stuff. That was a big deal back in the days before rock stars bit off the heads of bats onstage.

The most common thing was to bite the head off a live chicken. That was the standard Geek act in all the sideshows. But our Shawano Geek outstripped the others. He bit off the heads of fish, snakes, turtles, frogs, and rats. And he'd top off those meals with handfuls of roaches or maggots.

I've studied the whole Geek thing. It mostly comes down to something in people that makes them want to be disgusted. Something that makes them feel superior to those buggers in the jungle.

But there is something else to the Geek thing. Something that grabs us about blood dripping down someone's chin. There's a fear to that and an odd feeling too. Maybe because we all came out of savages who did such things.

I've talked to other people about this blood stuff. My grandson has studied psychology and he says we are always drawn to things that concern blood. And that's why we always have blood phobias.

He called the Geek "a white trash cousin to vampires." He sees it as a low-rent Dracula who doesn't scare us as much. That's because the Geek gets his blood from filthy sources and dirties himself.

The idea of filthy blood is a powerful thing. It makes us think of epidemic diseases. It even makes us think of the dangers of our carnal natures, what with AIDS and other things.

You combine that with the idea of overconsumption and gorging and it makes for a nightmarish image. Not only is there an appetite for polluted blood, but it is an addiction that can't be satisfied.

In a way, I think it's great that the Shawano Geek tricked people into thinking he was a jungle wild man. Everybody likes a local-boy-makes-good story. But it also makes the idea of Geeks scarier. When you know that it's not a matter of people from faraway places who we can think of as subhuman, then you know the Geeks are among us.

But isn't it good to know that? Isn't it better to keep the whole question on the table and out in the light? Isn't it better that there was a place for the Shawano Geek other than a locked room in the county home? Isn't it better that he didn't become an Ed Gein or Jeffrey Dahmer?

Cranberry Charlie

The marsh country across central Wisconsin holds many stories. Swamps, bogs, pothole lakes, and meandering streams mark a cultural and topographical transition zone between north country and farm country.

In some ways, this marsh country was the last frontier of Wisconsin. It lacked the pull of the good soils of the prairies and oak savannas of southern Wisconsin that drew the first wave of farmers. Absent were the massive tracts of prime timber that pulled the second wave of settlement to northern Wisconsin.

Marginal land often mandates marginal economic life. A few pockets of prosperity notwithstanding, opportunity and prosperity elude most of this area to this day.

One central Wisconsin success story that receives little notice outside the area is that of the cranberry industry. Even in Wisconsin, few know about the origins and development of this wetland fruit crop as a commercial mainstay.

Fewer still know about the bounty of folklore to be harvested in these damp fields. The hidden shacks on the sandy lanes shelter hardy souls who are in tune with the land and the seasons. They are often more connected to their past than their rural counterparts elsewhere.

This connection with the past has a personality focus that goes beyond the typical rural hero, to tell a story of a whole people. Marjorie, a Wood County widow, pours out the story as she fills large mugs with cola on a shaky deck outside her marshland mobile home.

🌾 🌾 🌾

If you really want to know the story of marshes, you have to learn about Cranberry Charlie.

Now there was a man who kept his promise to the people, a man who understood his duties to the elders. Someone who did something to improve the lives of the people and didn't spend all his time worrying about his share of the pot.

In order to understand how the Ho-Chunk produced a man like Cranberry Charlie, in spite of all the pressures and bad history, you

98

have to go back in time, back to when the Winnebago people first sold cranberries to the French over by Green Lake.

Among Indian people, often a family or clan has the duty to keep certain knowledge alive. They have the responsibility of preserving the practices and protecting all the things that go with a certain way of life. I can't tell you how it works or the names of the groups—that's a secret.

But Cranberry Charlie was from a family connected to the marshes. They had duties connected to those places that included the cranberries. They even said that one meaning for Ho-Chunk in old Hocak dialect was "cranberry people."

Cranberry Charlie was in that first generation of Ho-Chunk children sent away to boarding school. He ran away and hid with a clan leader in the marsh. He stayed there and learned the old ways until he came of age. Then he went on a long journey to learn the teachings of others.

He went out among the Indian people of New England, New Jersey, and Virginia. He spend time with the Seminoles in Florida and the Cajuns in Louisiana. He learned all there is to know about swamp life and life in general.

He learned many of the cranberry techniques back east. Things like growing the cranberries on dry bogs until harvest time and then flooding the bog in order to rake the berries. Things like using dikes and canals to control the bogs. Or like the removal of the peat moss in a new bog.

When he came back to Wisconsin he got the Ho-Chunk organized so that they could really dominate the cranberry industry. When the bogs were still public land, he made sure that Winnebago families got their claims staked out early at the prime locations.

When private investors started buying up the prime bogs, he kept the Winnebago linked into the new system. He taught the people all the skills so the growers could not operate without them. If you can imagine it, he managed to get the growers to pay for feasts and dances for their workers. The growers even paid for the harvest pow-wow.

Cranberry Charlie was most famous for his smarts. He was a big, strong man. But he is remembered because of the funny ways he had of tricking rich white people. A heavy and jolly man, he had a way of making people laugh even when he got the best of them.

He kept a lot of white squatters away from the Winnebago bogs with stories of spirits and demons. He had a great story about a spirit who told him when each bog was supposed to be harvested. He convinced the white bog owners that it was very bad luck to go against the spirit. In practical terms, it meant he could organize Winnebago migrant labor so it could be first on the spot when the "spirit" said it was time to harvest.

Some of the businessmen called him a medicine man. Some thought he was a wizard. But he really was more trickster and huckster than anything else. He really knew how to get people going, get them all worked up and moving exactly where he wanted them to go. He wasn't above hiring white helpers to do this.

He hired white con men all the time to make it seem like the Winnebago workers would get hired away. That would bid up the cost of labor. He hired phony pastors to come up and do revivals and cause observance of unheard of religious holidays. That's how the workers got breaks.

He hired a Polish woman from over by Stevens Point to dress up like a gypsy fortune teller. Any of the businessmen who crossed Cranberry Charlie would then have a public curse slapped on them. They really squirmed then.

He had a big bag of tricks. He exposed wrongdoing and injustice. He used public pressure and embarrassment. He even used blackmail when he had some real dirt on one of those big wheels.

Mostly, I remember him from stories that others told. But I do have a mental picture of him from when I was a child, when the people came out to the bogs to live in temporary villages of tents and shacks. Cranberry Charlie would stand there like a plantation overseer to look at the crowd.

He was quite a sight. He looked like a black mountain, what with his heavy body in a long dark rain slicker. The coat didn't even reach around him to button, so he wore a patchwork quilt vest under it. Around his neck was a cougar claw necklace from the last of the big swamp cats. On his head sat a wide brim black hat with a beaded band.

He looked like the grandfather of his people. And maybe that's what he was. He told us stories like a grandfather. He talked about the old days of handpicking the cranberries and taking them by boat to sell in the cities. He talked about the old Ho-Chunk ways.

But mostly he is remembered for his wish for everyone to be happy. He thought that a big belly laugh every day was better than anything a doctor could do for you.

At the end, the growers, brokers, and packers thought they put the joke over on Cranberry Charlie by making it so he and his people didn't qualify for social security. But the joke was on them. He had put away so many shipper and buyer kickbacks, so many labor crew finder's fees, and so many triple-dipping commissions, that he was able to live comfortably and help out many elders.

They say he died laughing. He was at the end anyway. But someone told him that a grower who refused to use Winnebago labor was wiped out by drought, disease, and cold weather. Even in his coffin, Cranberry Charlie's grin went from ear to ear.

102

PART TWO

Creature Feature—Wisconsin's Threatened and Threatening Species

Big Harry of Chequamegon

Stories about large furry manlike creatures are found through-out the world. Wisconsin has such tales in Walworth, Crawford, Monroe, Adams, Vilas, and Ashland counties.

Ashland County's Big Harry of Chequamegon is the only one of these stories that rivals those of the Himalayas' Abominable Snow-man or the Pacific Northwest's Bigfoot. In much of Wisconsin, as with the rest of North America, Bigfoot serves as the seeming inspi-ration for the accounts. Such stories have proliferated in the last several decades.

Big Harry of Chequamegon has far deeper roots going back over a hundred years. This suggests either a breeding group or unusual longevity. In Mellen, Mack, a retired pulp hauler, tells about Big Harry over morning coffee and doughnuts.

🌿 🌿 🌿

Big Harry of Chequamegon is what some professor called him years ago.

Most folks just call him Big Harry or Big Hairy. The Big Hairy is just a joke on his looks. Some think he's a rare animal. Others say he's half-human. A cross between a black bear and a Finn. Stands about seven foot, maybe four hundred pounds.

He's got dark brown hair over most of his body, a reddish-brown beard, and eyes as blue as Lake Superior in July. Big hands with thick fingers and thumbs. Feet about size eighteen with claws instead of toenails.

The story goes all the way back to old La Pointe County. In those days the county was made up of Ashland, Bayfield, and Douglas counties and the county seat was at La Pointe on Madeline Island. La Pointe County only lasted from 1845 to 1860 when Ashland County was created.

Some of the tales go all the way back to that time. That's when government surveyors were just starting to plat out the land. Big Harry would chase off many of those surveyors and other government men. He moved the monuments and markers that set off section lines. And he tossed at least one surveyor in Day Lake.

Now others claim that Big Harry goes back even further in time. They say that the Bad River Chippewa talked of a big creature that ran strangers out of the woods. And the Bad River people did figure in some of the lumber era stories.

Big Harry really started to make his reputation at the time of the big pine cutting, when the look of the Northwoods was changed forever. That came real late up this way compared to the pineries along the major rivers. Here we had to wait for the railroads.

The railroads were a part of those stories too. They and the logging operations went hand in hand. Big Harry did not like the clear cutting of the pine woods or the noisy trains. It was an invasion of his territory.

He met the challenge head-on. He scared the lumberjacks out of the woods and wrecked their camps. He harassed the crews laying the tracks and burned railroad stockpiles of ties. Big Harry pulled these tricks all over Ashland, Bayfield, and Iron counties, but he did have favorite territories.

The first was the route of the old Wisconsin Central Railroad. This ran up from Wausau through Butternut, Glidden, Mellen, and High Bridge to Ashland. Big Harry made it difficult for those towns to be settled. He ate milk cows and whole hogs during the night. These meals left a peculiar stench behind.

He threw logs at the passing trains. He smashed the old wooden cars, even caused some derailments.

Big Harry's second favorite location was up by Bad River on the reservation. He wasn't quite as disruptive there.

The J. S. Stearns Lumber Company had the government contract to log the reservation on the cheap and use Indian labor. But those Chippewa weren't nearly as dim as the Finns and Norskies. One sight of Big Harry and they all would just leave the woods for a few days.

My great-uncle Walter told me about some of the stranger stories here in Mellen. Big Harry had sort of a personal war with Mellen. Much of Big Harry's anger and disgust were directed at the old tannery in Mellen. Now there was a stinky and filthy place. Big Harry often tipped over the vats and set fire to the hides there.

The Mellen silver mine caught hell from him too. He must have learned to use dynamite 'cause the buildings out there blew up several times. I should mention that Big Harry more or less focused on mines once the pine cutting was done.

The sightings peaked around 1900 and dropped off after World War One. Oh, you'd hear that hunters would see him every so often. I saw him in 1957 when I was deer hunting near Mineral Lake.

But we did hear that Big Harry scared the crap out of some of the anti-treaty protesters who were harassing Indians at the boat landings. I guess he tossed a couple of those drunks into Clam Lake.

My nephew Frank told me last year he saw Big Harry following a core-drilling crew sent out by some mining company. Then last week he said he saw Big Harry petting one of those new bull elks.

Coon Valley Trolls

Norwegian Americans have kept troll stories alive in many parts of Wisconsin. The echoes of those stories resonate from Mt. Horeb's troll-lined streets to Norwegian festivals in Barron and Burnett counties.

While the troll as an object of Old World cultural appreciation is very alive, it is far rarer to hear of active trolls in North America. Accounts of trolls were common in the logging camps of nineteenth-century Minnesota and Wisconsin. Sightings were particularly numerous along the St. Croix River.

The Coon Valley trolls stand out from other troll stories because of their early roots and continued vitality. One could stop in the Vernon County community dozens of times and never hear any mention of trolls. Then a single stop for a cold beer after an unseasonably hot ride up Highway 14 might put you with a sleep-deprived white-haired man on a bar stool.

🌿 🌿 🌿

Hot as the hinges of Hell, eh?

Who can sleep in this weather? Who'd want to do anything other than sip beer and stay close to the air conditioner?

Yeah, there's lots of sleepless people around here, what with the heat and the moving around at night.

The old people always said the trolls moved about in these hot summer nights. The trolls always are most active in July and August. They really get going right around summer solstice.

In the Scandinavian stories trolls were most active up near the Arctic Circle on those short nights when it barely got dark at all. Those old Scandinavians said the trolls caused the Northern Lights and made the reindeer run away.

People have all sorts of strange notions about trolls. They tend to think of funny-looking men who look like Snow White's dwarves and live under porches.

They're just about the opposite. Trolls are giants. Remnants of a race of giants that lived in the northern lands before today's people.

They speak Old Norse or something close to Icelandic. Some say they were originally born out of Iceland's volcanoes. That's why they're fond of caves. They come from the bowels of the Earth. Not from under porches or pig pens. Not from under bridges either. Well, maybe under a bridge as a temporary hiding place.

The Coon Valley trolls are a bit different than the Old Country ones. A little less nasty. Not stealing babies like they did in Norway.

Our trolls followed Helgar Gilronson over from Norway. He was the first Town of Coon settler in 1848.

Peter Olsen took three of our trolls with him when he enlisted with Company A, Wisconsin Thirty-fourth Infantry in the Civil War. All those Union Army Irish and German sergeants didn't think much about three more big ugly Norwegians out on night sentry duty.

For years this history of trolls was taught in the red brick Coon Valley school. It was part of the family history of the Andersons, Martinsons, and Holgersons.

Our five trolls live in a hidden cave up Coon Creek in Spring Coulee. Their range these days runs through the towns of Christiana, Coon, and Hamburg.

They have five distinct personalities. There's the farmer, the hunter, the fisherman, the woodsman, and the blacksmith. They're sort of patron saints in reverse. They curse humans in those activities.

The farmer dries up cows and spooks the chickens. In the old days he would make the horses mighty flighty. The hunter scares the game away. It's said that game is nowhere to be found the day after one of his nighttime walks.

The fisherman wades local creeks on hot summer nights. You can see fish floating belly up the next day. The woodsman goes around the woods at night laying booby traps. His idea of a joke is a woodlot full of deadfalls, top snags, and widowmakers.

The blacksmith tampers with tools and mechanical things. If your hoe, rake, and shovel handles break off in midsummer you'll know he's been around.

If you're foolishly out and about at night you might see them and you'll certainly smell their stinking sweat. They're all big and ugly, but with slightly different individual looks.

The farmer has huge baggy one-strapped overalls. The hunter has a leather vest. The fisherman has short pants. The woodsman carries an axe. The blacksmith wears a leather apron and has a bright red beard.

It's this last one I've seen closest. He smells like sulfur. His eyes glow like red coals. His beard even seems like iron filing sparks are flying off of it. On hot nights he sneaks around my place. Mostly out in the shed. But he will sometimes peek in on the Old Lady when she's in the tub.

110

I read up on these things. If we could only corner them until day-light the sun would turn them into stone. If we planned it right we could catch them in a bunch right along Highway 14 and have a little wayside park. We could make a few bucks off of them!

Watertown's Elbedritzel

Wisconsin's diverse European American groups brought many references to Old Country mythical animals them to North America.

Tales of dragons, unicorns, and such usually retain their Old Country setting. The magic flowing from first-hand accounts is missing when the storyteller cannot speak intimately of places and people.

Only a few of Wisconsin's European mythological animals physically traveled with the immigrants and set up housekeeping in the pioneer settlements. Watertown's Elbedritzel stands out among these as representing old legends, traditions of humor, and rites of passage.

The custodian of this story exhibits deep appreciation for its cultural roots. Join Catherine in her antique shop as she dusts off stoneware and stories.

🌿 🌿 🌿

Not many young people today would know about the Elbedritzel.

Fewer still would realize that the story must be approached on two levels, as a mystical experience and as a joke. On the mystical level the Elbedritzel has deep roots. It is part of that tradition of mythical birds that includes the Auspices, Harpies, Rocs, and Sirens, only a bit more benign.

Elbedritzels are generally omens of good luck. They are associated with finding wealth or love. They might also make an appearance at the end of long suffering. They are not physically intimidating like many of the mythical birds. They're rarely larger than a turkey. As strange as it sounds, they combine elements of peacocks and kiwis.

Elbedritzels are definitely Germanic in origin. They're also referred to as Elbedritsches, Ebbetritts, and Elfedrins. But they're not generally talked about in German American heritage circles where university-trained values hold sway. No, Elbedritzels are of peasant stock. They are creatures of rural areas and small towns.

In Watertown they were part of the divisions between the various groups of Germans that settled here. The Elbedritzels were best known by the Rhineland families that farmed south of town toward Ebenezer. On the other hand the clergy and teacher families from places like Frankfurt and Dresden initially knew next to nothing about the bird.

But word of the Elbedritzel did spread around from the 1850s up to the 1890s. By then we had a genuine German American culture that combined the old regional elements.

Our Turnerverein, or athletic club, had an Elbedritzel emblem at its founding in 1860. The old newspapers *Weltburger, Anzieger,* and *Volkszeitung* carried Elbedritzel stories.

Now the real problem with the Elbedritzel is not only are they hard to find and hard to see but they can be seen only by the pure of heart. Children often see them as do the simple souls among us.

This is where the jokes and our little traditions come in. It's connected to the German love of the hunt. The old men of Watertown loved to talk the new teachers or clergy into accompanying them on Elbedritzel hunts. This was our version of the southern snipe hunt.

My father would usually take the uninitiated out to the Mud Lake marsh and set them up in a blind. Then he would just leave them out there in the dark. Next morning they'd be madder than wet cats. But no young man in those days could be fully accepted into adult circles without enduring the late night Elbedritzel hunt.

The Elbedritzel also figured in other local supernatural tales. One was about the ghost of a murdered French trader. The Elbedritzel preceded the ghost sightings.

The other story was about the Indian burial ground in the old Third Ward. A whole flock of Elbedritzels was seen there. So they must have some magical properties.

We ladies were of course denied many of the pleasures of the Elbedritzel hunts. The old men did not see fit to take us out to the marsh.

But never mind that. It's hard to imagine women abandoning each other in a dark swamp. No, we had our own Elbedritzel hunts. Ours were timed to the spring flowers and apple blossoms.

Instead of the bogs and swamps, we repaired to the meadows and woods. There we young girls set up twilight watch for this "bird of love." Yes, we thought it was a romantic omen. Whoever saw it first was next to wed, bear strong children, and be happy.

And we lured it in a romantic way. No off-key duck calls and moldy cheese in gunny sacks like the men. We used the soft singing of love songs to draw the Elbedritzel in close. Then we used a bowl of early wild violet petals as bait. This brought them up into clearings.

Our Elbedritzel hunts were different from the men's. We saw the Elbedritzel!

The Willy Wooly of Kidrick Swamp

Mysterious creatures often inspire conflicting reports. Collectors of such tales must endure various claims about size, color, and habits. Yet stories of things lurking in the woods or hills usually produce some common reference points. The words bearlike *and* apelike *are common in this genre.*

Local sources also tend to have shared assumptions about the origins and behaviors that at least provide a framework for classification. It is rare indeed when those familiar with a creature cannot agree on the simplest of questions.

Taylor County presents such a rarity. Payton, a U.S. Forest Service employee, has studied the various accounts with a scientist's thoroughness.

🌿 🌿 🌿

Perhaps it will take years and years of fitting pieces together.

For twenty-two years I've listened to the stories, combed through the old newspapers, and studied zoological journals. See, at first I

thought this "thing" was an escaped exotic animal, maybe a giant tree sloth or something of that type. Or maybe someone had dumped it off along a back road.

But then I could see that the stories went too far back for that. Keeping exotics as pets is a pretty recent phenomenon. So then I thought about circus and carnival escapees. You know, a lot of circuses headquartered in Wisconsin, some as far north as Merrill, with all manner of sideshows, freak shows, and performing animals.

But that avenue never turned up anything other than temporary escapes. You know the drill. Tiger escapes. Deputy sheriffs corner it in calf barn. Tiger full of holes. Or even more common, kangaroo escapes. Hops away into the woods. Freezes to death. Trapper finds frozen carcass in a marsh with varmints chewing on it.

The stories went further back than the circus era. Some of the older stories went back to the main logging era. Those loggers saw something, but they never called it much more than a thing, or maybe the Jump River thing.

My Ojibwe friends at Lac Court Oreilles say the story goes way back for them, too. But even there they have no solid agreement. For some it's a monster, for others a spirit, for still others, a remnant of an almost extinct species. I gave them a hard time on this stuff. I asked them why the thing wasn't mentioned in the treaties or in Judge Crabb's decisions.

So after a whole lot of fussing and jawing, I still didn't have anything to call this creature. Nothing to label the growing file. So I thought, what the hell, these guys who discover comets or rare plants get to name them. Shoot, most of the time they name the things after themselves. But I ruled out using my name. Too many letters and too hard to pronounce. Besides, why blame the thing on the Poles? So I was stuck with the name quandary for a long time. At least until I had my first sighting.

Now, you might think that would have cleared things up for me, or at least brought them into better focus. But it didn't. I had been researching for over ten years before I had a sighting myself. Just south of the Jump River lookout.

Just a glimpse, a blur. You know how it is on a bright day when you're in a woods and something passes quickly through a shaft of light and into the shadows?

I still can hardly believe what I saw. A lot of reddish-brown fur, wool-like, dragging on the ground in some places. Just a hint of horn on the head. Kind of a reptile's belly. A bit of suggestion of rhinoceros armor plating on the sides. A long dragging hairless tail. Intelligent, almost curious big yellow eyes. A roundish, puckered mouth.

My seven-year-old daughter had a book about a strange creature called a "willy." So we added on the wooly feature and linked it to its chief habitat. That's how we came up with "Willy Wooly of Kidrick Swamp."

The Willy Wooly is still out there. We get a report from a hunter almost every year. It's really surprising that it hasn't been shot in deer season.

It's a lot of fun to hear those reports. One will say there's a llama out there. The next will call it a furry alligator. Or a giant horned possum. One guy even thought it might be a cross between a hippo and a musk ox.

Up here we kind of learn to live and let live. The darn ugly thing ain't hurting anything. So what's the problem?

The Sprague Stumper-Jumper

Larger-than-life human characters pop up in almost every corner of Wisconsin. Strange creatures are also widely distributed. Spirit shape-shifting is present in many American Indian stories.

Juneau County has a story that combines all three elements and is thus difficult to classify. Is heroic action the criterion for inclusion in the human category? Do crude animal habits require placement in the creature classification? Does a hint of the supernatural consign a story to the realm of spirit stories?

There are no easy answers to such questions. Folklore is often harmed by a tendency to overclassify and analyze. Folktales are filled with themes—visible and subterranean—that layer meanings as thick as all of human history and psychology allow. Yet, on the most basic level, stories just are.

In the end, my evaluation of the story forces placement in the creature category—an imperfect outcome, but one at least partially justified by what the story is not. It is not a hero in the sense of organic connection to a community or way of life; it is not of the people. Its supernatural dimensions do not flow from established spiritual tradition; it does not represent the soul of any particular group.

Perhaps someone else will intuitively know other elements to this story. Perhaps a winter evening with a bottle of Barneveld Botham wine and a textbook on Jung will promote keener insight. Perhaps not.

Maybe the meaning lies in the rambunctious style of my source. Maybe it relates to the lonely stretches of Juneau County inhabited by the object of the story. Maybe it is the references to the abandoned lands and the encroaching wilderness. Maybe not.

But the story does serve as a good example of what can happen when a person who spends much of his time hidden away in the woods and marshes goes into town. An exchange occurs. The woodsman gets supplies and the townsmen get some stories. It is a Wisconsin process that is as old as La Baye, La Pointe, and Prairie du Chien.

Listen to Marvin, the wiry man with the gray beard stubble, as he leans on the counter at the Necedah hardware store.

🌱 🌱 🌱

My neighbor saw the Sprague Stumper-Jumper again.

Lots of people thought the porky critter was dead or had moved on. Ha! You get that type of empty talk from people whose idea of spending time with nature is their walk to the mailbox.

If you haven't heard of the Stumper-Jumper before, well, let me educate you. It's half-man, half-pig. No, I'm not pulling your thing! No kidding!

How did it get to be? Where did it come from? What does it want? Darn if I know. Greater minds than mine have ciphered on those questions. Well, I can guess on the last one. The darn thing wants to be left alone.

I had an old boy try to tell me it was a hybrid. Yeah, an actual cross between a pig and a human. He said those old bachelor farmers on those sandy marsh farms got mighty lonely back in the thirties. Wonder what Jimmy Dean the Sausage King would say about that?

Another old fellow told me it was a Winnebago who spent the winter in a pigpen eating corn and slop. He just gradually turned piglike. The guy was an Indianhater, so you can't buy that story.

But a Ho-Chunk lady told me something that sounded more likely. She said it was like in those Greek stories. You know, in the old days they had half-man, half-horse creatures and men with bulls' heads on them.

She said it was probably from a curse. Probably from a witch. Probably was a good-looking fellow and then he got the witchy lady mad. I tell you, some of these old bags in the swamps can turn on you pretty mean if you drink their milk and don't end up buying the cow!

So he's kind of a sad bugger. Kind of like what you think about with those hunchback or beauty and the beast stories. He's really not scary to look at, just different. We got lots around here that won't be doing beauty commercials any time soon!

But he's lucky he's out in the wild where he's seldom seen. Otherwise someone would probably shoot him or trap him. More than once the town drunks talked about getting him in a cage and hauling him to the carnivals. But that would take more energy and more smarts than those knuckleheads have ever seen.

I could do it and I've had my chances. But it wouldn't be right. I mean, the porker is half-human. I mean, we've got people dumber than stones in this town who've got constitutional rights. We've got a no-brain kid who steals the same darn thing five times, gets caught

five times, and five times gets a taxpayer-paid lawyer. And we should shoot somebody 'cause they got a snout on their puss?

Maybe they're all worked up because of the magic stuff. Yeah, they say the bugger changes from one thing to another. Horse hockey! The only thing I've seen change about him is his clothes. Ripped overalls in the summer—no shirt or shoes—and a denim coat and barn boots in the winter.

Some chuckleheads say they seen him turn into other types of animals. Some say he can be totally pig one time and totally man another time. I don't buy it! Those are the same people who go "whoops," after their dead buck turns out to be a doe or their brother-in-law.

Yeah, there was one time that the pig story had more to it. One old marsh biddy who's especially fond of me saw a pig out at Goose Pool. But she didn't see any change. Just a pig. That's harder to explain. Fifty years ago people kept pigs. I don't know of any now.

The Stumper-Jumper just loves those back lanes. Our hidden spots. No area's got more long, lonely, fern-lined dirt lanes through jack pine and popple. Lots of places to get lost out there. Lots of rumors of bodies hidden out there. The owls, the ospreys, the sharp-tailed grouse, and the Stumper-Jumper are the only eyes out there.

He lives out of cabins and shacks in such places. That's where his food comes from. That's where his clothes come from too. He knows the schedule of those weekend people. They don't seem to mind the few things that are missing. But I almost peppered his butt with bird-shot after he took my overalls off the backyard washline!

And chewing tobacco too! He loves to chew. Anytime I've set down a pouch of Red Man on a stump, a log, or a pickup fender, the thing is gone as soon as I turn around.

One time he got my tobacco when I was cutting jack pine. I was hopping mad and I yelled into the brush. All I got for my trouble was about a pint of tobacco spit on the top of my head. I couldn't even see the bugger!

There's one thing about the Stumper-Jumper that I don't under-stand. That's his watching out for the ladies. Yeah, he's done quite a few rescues in his time. Young chickies and old hags.

Mostly stuff like pushing them out of ditches without even a howdy-do. But there's been serious stuff too. Stuff like carrying one very hefty lady out of a burning farmhouse. Other times he's run off troublemakers who were bothering women who live alone.

Some even say that he comforts widows in the fullest meaning of the word. They say you can tell the next day if the old gal comes to town and instead of her hunched little shuffle walk, she's got a little spring in her step and sway in her hips!

But I don't know about that. It doesn't fit. When he helps a gal, he's gone before she can thank them. He seems to put a high price on his privacy. Maybe it's different after dark. Maybe he likes to be thanked privately!

But the back lanes are emptying out. I don't think we'll see many more women out there. It won't be long before the men are out of the back lanes too.

For sixty years the place has been emptying out. You can't even see where the farms used to be. I can show you dozens of old homesteads where you can't even find a foundation. Even a lot of the hunting shacks built right after World War Two have rotted down into moss beds.

When it's all gone, when we're all gone, then I guess the Stumper-Jumper belongs to the weekenders. What becomes of him then?

The Giant Brown Swiss

Bovine references pepper Wisconsin vocabulary with earthy and pungent aromas. Bon mots and folksy customs link us to cows in the national consciousness. From T-shirt slogans like SMELL OUR DAIRY AIR, to cow-chip throwing contests, to the ever-present cheesehead, we find these large milk-producing animals in every part of our state's identity.

Cow stories are not rare. Loosen up the tongue of any rural old-timer and you will find a wealth of cow tales: lost cows, rampaging cows, cows as dowry, cows going to market, feral cows, and so on. My prior story collection efforts even turned up one ghost herd of cows ("Lime Ridge Cows," Driftless Spirits).

The cow as story object serves many different functions. One can also detect changes in these functions depending on the time frame of the story.

The stories set in the pioneer era focused on the solitary "Old Bossie." The cow often made the trek with the pioneer family and had a crucial role in the self-sufficient household economy. It had an individual personality and status equivalent to the family homestead horse.

After the railroads made it possible to transport milk and cheese, the herds grew to twenty or thirty cows. In those stories, the emphasis is shifted to "milking time," which replaced the light chore of milking one cow with an organized family endeavor.

Today dairying features industrialization, technology, and such auxiliary figures as dairy inspectors, credit agency representatives, and university extension agents. These authority figures emerged in the 1980s sub-genre of "foreclosure lore."

The cow also emerges as a symbol of power and mystery in some stories. Rescue cows lead lost children home or save humans from exposure through their warmth. Life source cows suckle other species.

But as prevalent as cows are on the Wisconsin landscape, there is also a lament for our "lost" cows. The popular black and white Holstein has displaced the cornucopia of cow breeds that once sustained family homesteads. Thus, we can talk about "rare" cows in the Dairy State.

In Green County, in the Town of Cadiz, Eli, a former herdsman, knows of such matters.

🐄 🐄 🐄

Did you ever hear of the Giant Brown Swiss?

It was the biggest cow that ever lived. Bigger than any cow P. T. Barnum ever came up with. Bigger than anything that you'd see in any rodeo or livestock show.

It had the height of the biggest draft horses and weighed over five thousand pounds. It was thicker than a rhinoceros. The legs were as thick as utility poles. And, *ach*, what a head. It took a half bushel of oats in one mouthful.

It was a sight to behold. Just looking at it could set you to shivering. It was like you were in church. It just made you feel little to be near it. A bit like when you go to one of those city museums and you're next to one of those big old skeletons of things that died off long ago.

Not many people ever saw the Giant Brown Swiss. But I did. I worked its barn as a youngster. I worked for her owner.

He kept her hidden. He was a funny man that way. He was an old Swiss fellow who thought he could breed Swiss cows up past Holstein size. If he could do that—breed a large cow and still keep the Swiss buttermilk content—well, he would be a rich man. So, it was the money that kept him going.

He looked all over the country to find the biggest bulls and biggest cows to breed. It took him only about thirty years to breed up to the big one I'm talking about.

He used an old horse barn on the back part of the farm where no one would see. The Giant Brown Swiss was the only cow he kept in

121

there. He had to knock out the stall dividers because it took up two horse stall widths.

Ach, the pride. It was all about pride. Pride over the size. Pride over the rich cream. Pride over the pedigree. Pride over having a thing that no one else had and having such a big secret.

Some of that pride even rubbed off on those of us who worked with her. We did things no one else had ever done. We first milked her into a washtub that was up on rollers. Later, we milked into four milk cans on a cart—one teat for each can.

We milked from a chair on wheels because a stool was too low. We needed the wheels so we could coast around the other side of the udder. You had to milk each teat with two hands. A boy or a short man could milk under her standing up.

And the manure. What a job! You could fit the wheelbarrow right between her hind legs. You had to empty it about every two hours.

But that pointed out the biggest problem with the Giant Brown Swiss. She wasn't an efficient feed converter. She needed high quality forage. Our old style Timothy hay wasn't enough so we had to grain her. That made for expensive milk. In the end, that bankrupted the old Swiss fellow. All the special care and food made it an expensive proposition.

This is what happens when you don't understand the true nature of a thing. You take it past its limits and you end up tricking yourself that you've accomplished something.

We lose sight of the fact that the Earth was created with everything we need right on it. Each animal and plant with a special role to play. It's natural for humans to tinker around. But the old Swiss fellow found out what happens when you go too far.

We've ignored our inheritance. Do you know that there were once dozens of cow breeds? Oh, you still hear about Brown Swiss and Jersey. But what about Ayrshire, Guernsey, Milking Shorthorn, Dutch Belted, Dexter, and Canadian? Even beef breeds like Simmental gave good milk.

Then the other animals. *Ach*, the sheep, the hogs, the horses, and poultry. Hundreds of kinds, each with its own special traits. Low fat meat, long wool, heat tolerance, or ability to graze on poor land. Then there's disease resistance and ability to handle rough conditions. But we're letting all this fade away.

We made the Holstein too big. Now it lives on antibiotics. Our cows live in stress. Now we give them hormones so they'll produce even more. And we forget that whatever we do to our animals we are doing to ourselves.

The cow should teach us to go slow, chew slowly, and sit in the shade and digest things. We have interfered with animals for thousands of years. But it was always slow, over many generations.

Now our science moves quicker. *Ach*, they can reach right into the genes. Maybe that's too much like playing God. And when man plays God, well, that's like a kid without a license driving a big truck on a crowded highway.

I say let the breeds stay as they are until we have more answers. They all have something to offer. And we don't even know what yet.

We don't have to make the cow bigger. It's as big as it was meant to be. The cow is Mother Earth by my way of looking at it. It's our most basic source of nourishment. It's our symbol for something. Those Egyptians and others worshipped cows. The cow is a giant without any help from us.

The Little Hodag

Rare and mythical creatures have a long history in Wisconsin. Perhaps no other category does as much to blur the line between folklore and fakelore. *Cynical observers might say that therein lies a distinction without a difference.*

But for folklorists, ethnographers, and phenomenologists, it is more complicated than that. Does the story have local roots, cultural benchmarks, and a multi-generational tradition? Or is it a contemporaneous fabrication calculated to defraud or delight?

There is also the whole question of separating out "myth" from "reality." The American Indians in Wisconsin give us a rich legacy of storied creatures that European Americans seldom see. Is a creature real when it evolves out of a collective subconscious and manifests itself in a collective conscious and the material culture?

Finally, there are murky folklore swamps of psychology and unexplained happenings. The first is a bog rich with possible meanings. The second is a quivering muck of the inexplicable. How many of our story traditions derive from our fear of the unknown?

The Hodag story provides the framework for many of the European American tales of creatures in Wisconsin. This creature of the Northwoods has a long tradition that is counterbalanced with hoaxes, earnest sightings, and civic boosterism (in the form of emblems, mascots, and at least one hodagburger).

The Hodag tale has been told so many times that it could not bear retelling here were it not for my source's extensive knowledge of the creature and his presentation of new information. Join me as I pull over at a Highway 13 wayside near Park Falls. There, a rotund fellow is selling berries and woven baskets out of the back of his truck. Big Dave throws in the stories for free.

🌿 🌿 🌿

The old Hodags are dead!

My granddad was from over by Rhinelander, so we were brought up on Hodag stories. He saw the last big one die north of Antigo.

Yup, he was a believer in them all his life and did all he could to straighten out the b.s. and distortions that other people tacked on. I guess you could say I'm carrying on the family tradition.

The whole Hodag story is a messed up deal. It's so goofed up you'd think the legislature down in Madison was in charge of it. It's not often such a simple story gets turned butt upwards—unless you count religion.

If you sort it out, you find that there *was* such a rare creature. Then you have some scam artists blow it up into something else, pull a sideshow hoax, and make some money off of it. That discredits the whole story. Next, the big breed dies off in northeast Wisconsin, so of course no one can find a specimen.

Gard and Sorden in *Wisconsin Lore* call that breed the Black Hodag or Bovinus Spiritualis. It should have been called the Great Hodag or Bovinus Spiritualis Maximus. They're all dead now.

124

Those writer fellows got it about half right, but you can tell that they were poking fun at the whole thing by throwing the Hodag in with made-up and distorted creatures.

Wisconsin Lore lists twenty-nine rare creatures of the Wisconsin Northwoods. And for verification they cite the lying sack of bear turds that made up the story about Paul Bunyan's camp being in the Onion River country. Onion River camp, my buttcheeks! Paul Bunyan only used that spot as a toilet. Everyone knows his real camp was near Park Falls on the Flambeau River.

That spread a lot of misinformation. It created a belief that the only place you could find such things in Wisconsin was in that corner of the state. It elevated the status of some stories that were simply logging camp hallucinations resulting from bad corn liquor. And it lumped into the fanciful category some things that should have been investigated more closely.

Some of those toxic alcohol visions came out as sightings of Hangdowns, Hidebehinds, and Pumptifusels. If there were any real creatures behind those tales it was simply a matter of drunk lumberjacks seeing a Hodag.

On the other hand, there were things like the Gumberoo and the Luferlang that had something behind them. At least like the Hodag, you had earlier Indian stories of something similar that provided partial corroboration.

But all this confusion did nothing but cover up the fact that there were two Hodag breeds and that one of them survived. That's right, Bovinus Spiritualis Minimus, the Lesser or Little Hodag.

Most of them run about collie size. By the way, they love to eat collies, but they subsist mainly on stray cats and rabbits. A baby of this breed is about cat size, and a few old ones might get close to a hundred pounds if they have a steady food supply.

The Great Hodag was not as big as the stories made it out to be. Mostly they were in the bear-size range—that's what they were often taken for in the dark woods. Oh, I heard of an eight-hundred-pounder once, but who knows? The stories and the big hoax made them out to be the size of dumptrucks.

Now with the Little Hodag, there are signs that they are becoming more accustomed to humans. Sort of like the coyotes on the edges of cities. But they're still seldom seen because no one is looking for them.

On top of that, they're a threatened, if not endangered, species. Like their bigger extinct cousins, they were hunted and trapped without mercy. But the Little Hodag, being a smaller and more elusive target, is making a partial comeback. Some say it's because hunters and trappers thought the Little Hodag was just at the puppy stage and so they left them to grow.

There is a lot of confusion about what a Hodag looks like and what its habits add up to. That goes back to the hoax and sideshow.

They are carnivorous. But unlike the hoaxers, I'd never say they eat human flesh. I know for sure that the Little Hodag doesn't. And the Great Hodag never killed people. They just picked on some frozen lumberjack carcasses during sparse feed conditions during some really bad winters.

The Great Hodag lived in the dense swamps of Oneida and Vilas counties. The Little Hodag was pretty much the same way over here in Price, Iron, and Ashland counties. But now it's turned to culverts, abandoned farm buildings, and tumbled-down hunting shacks. The surviving Little Hodags range throughout the Chequamegon National Forest and down to Ladysmith.

As far as what it looks like, it's pretty much like the Great Hodag. Just a little lighter in color in the summer and kind of a silver gray in winter. But it has the characteristic spearlike tail, spikes along the spine, shaggy hair, two horns, and short but powerful legs. Kind of a souped-up armadillo on steroids.

Old Menominees told my granddad that there were once lots of Indian stories about the Hodag. But I've been over to Keshena to ask and all they could tell me is the Rhinelander Chamber of Commerce story.

In this neck of the woods, it's a little different. The Chippewa tell me stories—when they're not spearing *my* fish—about strange creatures in the woods. Some of them sound like Little Hodags.

But I think those Chippewa are on to something you should check out. They say that things like the Hodag can take many shapes. So one minute it's a Hodag, the next minute it's a lynx, and the next it's a thing not seen in ten thousand years. Some even tell me it could be the gal who appeared out of nowhere on her Harley and took me to a mobile home for two days.

The whole point is that there's a wild spirit in these things. It runs through the accounts of all the rare creatures. That wild spirit *is* Wisconsin.

Porte des Morts Wiitiko

Anishinabe and Algonquin stories refer to a race of cannibal giants that seem to be survivors of the last ice age. Ojibwe stories refer to the Wendigo, Wendeeko, and Windigo. Other Algonquin tribes have different names for this monster made of ice.

The stories of the displaced tribes like the Ottawa, Sac, and Potawatomi were harder to track. But here and there, individuals or small groups stayed behind and intermarried with European Americans. Thus, a few stories survived in odd spots and with families with complex pedigrees.

The story below geographically relates to the passage between the Door County peninsula and Washington Island. However, as a bit of hereditary lore, it belongs to a large extended family on Sturgeon Bay.

A variety of ethnic currents in that family serve only to enrich this tale told by Basil, a retired boatbuilder.

127

You won't find many people around here who will tell you Indian stories.

You can look at lots of them and tell they have more Indian blood than me. But they have no appreciation of hybrid status that comes from my Danish, French, Belgian, Polish, Irish, Potawatomi, and Ottawa background.

My great-uncle Harald told me that one family lived out at Sherwood Point right up to when the settlers came. They were a mixed Potawatomi and Ottawa family who had been traders. They had moved out of bark huts and built log houses like the settlers.

They were the storytellers of the family. They had stories about everything. How the whitefish came to be in the lake. How people came to invent boats. How the deer came down from the stars.

Pretty much true to the Indian stories I've heard. Well, with bits of Viking stuff, saints, and Grimm's fairy tales thrown in.

The strangest story had to be what they called the Wiitiko up at Porte des Morts. When we were kids, the idea of an ice monster living in that choppy channel scared the bejeebers out of us.

Now, the usual Indian legends of this kind talk about a giant iceman who eats people and gets bigger and hungrier as he eats them. Some of the stories you hear around Lake Superior talk about the monsters coming into being only in winter. Up in Canada, it was thought that they ate only idiots and cripples. Kind of a tool for survival of the fittest.

Our Wiitiko must come from the same background. But he's got something about him that I've never heard before. He was active year-round. Came up out of the channel about anytime he wanted to, although a lot of encounters were at night.

Also, he doesn't eat whole villages like the ones up north. He seems to focus on bad actors and people from Illinois in big boats. During the Depression, he went after a lot of fish poachers and guys who stole out of the fishing nets of other people. I guess he broke up the boats of those big fish-poaching rings that supplied the Chicago black market.

The Wiitiko has a big connection to fish and fishing. It's connected in an odd way to fishing luck. Right after he is seen, the fishing always gets better. The flip side is that if he hasn't stirred for a while, the fishing is lousy.

Weather is a big tie-in too. I guess the old Indians used him almost like a barometer. If he did one thing or another it meant certain types

128

of weather systems or wind shifts. But all that precise knowledge is lost now.

The stories said a bad spell of weather brought on sightings of the Wiitiko, especially those nasty fall storms that whip out of the northeast. But then, after he was seen, things would usually get pretty calm.

At one time, it was almost like having an almanac, back when people knew what they were looking for. Then there were signs that connected the Wiitiko to the phases of the moon and the seasons.

You might say that this connection between the Wiitiko and the elements went back to the time when this part of the Earth was shaped. It was passed down that these ice monsters were spawned out of glaciers. That's why the lake country in the middle of the U.S. and Canada had so many.

They say that the Sun disappeared for a time. Then the Darkness put a blanket of snow on Mother Earth and lay with her. The children of this odd coupling were the Wiitiko. There's a significance to this idea of a being made of frozen water. Deep waters represent the soul. Water is the chief element of life.

Our Wiitiko has a history of involvement in human affairs that you don't hear about up north. Especially how he figured in some Potawatomi history. You probably know about how there was a big war against the Potawatomi three or four hundred years ago. The enemy tribe had pushed them out of Michigan, and then pursued them up the Fox River and eventually forced a last stand on Washington Island.

The enemies prepared to launch hundreds of canoes in an attack. They even set out across Porte des Morts. But the waves got higher and the wind got stiffer. The missionaries who first recorded the story of the battle said that a storm claimed the enemy canoes. But I think they were working off the Spanish Armada story.

My Indian ancestors said the Wiitiko rose out of the channel and swallowed those canoes. That's right, chomped down wood, spears, arrows, and hundreds of tribal enemies without so much as a belch.

Trempealeau's Buffabob Herd

*W*isconsin has its share of odd animals. Many are the remnants
of large pre-Ice Age populations that sought refuge in the driftless area.
Almost all of these creatures are things of the night or things of hidden
places. The majority are elusive and seldom seen except by hunters
and loggers.

Often the stories of such animals are themselves limited to small
circles resolved to avoid publicity. Those privileged to glimpse rare
creatures feel proprietary toward them.

So it is extremely uncommon to encounter someone who has a plan
for future notoriety and commercialization of a rare creature. Ida
is a crusty Centerville farm wife whose profane remarks must be
heavily edited.

🌿 🌿 🌿

The way I look at it, something's useless unless ya can make a
_____ dollar off it.

We got all these farmers who've wasted years yanking cow tits
and don't have jack _____! Only a man could figure out a way to work
twelve _____ hours a day, seven _____ days a week and still not make
a _____ cent! I'll tell ya, bringing a woman onto a dairy farm is a _____
form of domestic abuse!

These _____ for brains men around here can't even recognize a gold mine when they got one. I mean the _____ _____ _____ _____ buffabobs! Hell, we got the corner on the whole _____ supply!

I betcha ya never seen a buffabob, have ya? Well, when we're done shooting the _____ we'll go out to the barn. I got four out there right now.

The buffabob is a _____ cousin to the buffalo. Most likely a buffalo-mountain goat hybrid. The males have _____ spiral, straight-up horns like a goat. They're shaggy like buffalo and got buffalo size. The females give rich milk—if you get them to stand still in the stanchion.

The meat is real tasty too! The whole thing is like prime rib. But less fat. Even the males have sweet meat if you cut their _____ off.

Buffabobs have run wild around here ever since the first settlers came. For years there was a big herd down at Perrot State Park. The _____ herd had the run of the wildlife refuge down there.

Eventually people figured out that buffabobs could be domesticated. Hell, it ain't easy to get a halter on the _____, but they'll come to rattling corn in a bucket.

It was our secret around here for a long time. Eventually we started a breed association to improve the genetics and keep out the _____ riff-raff.

When we knew we had enough to spare, we started the annual Trempealeau buffabob roast. No _____ outsiders allowed in for that!

We developed our own management plan for the wild ones too. Eventually we had to have a hunting season to control the wild population. The _____ cause a lot of damage. They eat crops and even the _____ laundry off the washline! It's that _____ goat part!

We get two _____ thousand dollars a head from trophy hunters who fly in to pop them. Hell, we got three thousand from some _____ _____ rock star bow hunter!

It's working out pretty good. Think of the _____ mess the _____ DNR could made of it. It would be like the _____ deer situation.

Now ya probably wonder how we can get away with all this without the government coming down on us. Well, we're a bit off the beaten track. Plus, those dumb _____ couldn't find their own _____ with a flashlight.

The younger generation tells me there's tons of _____ pot grown around here. Some right under the nose of the law. They can't find that either.

So we got to market this quietly. I've got the plan to start with the natural food stores and the Twin Cities restaurants.

We got a little rumor cooked up to boost sales. We started a neat little _____ story that the meat makes you lose weight, clears up your complexion, acts as tonic against infection, and boosts your sex life.

We're gonna made buffabob hair sweaters for the natural fiber crowd. We gotta contract for buffabob leather vests and cowboy boots—with the likeness of your favorite country and western singer embossed right on the _____!

We're even gonna sell the _____ ground-up horn to the Chinese!

The Dwarf Mastodons of Boaz

Farmers and university researchers periodically turn up bones from the large elephantlike creatures that once roamed North America.

The bones answer many questions about the lives and habits of that long-extinct species. Occasional discoveries of frozen carcasses in melting glaciers round out the picture.

Why did the mastodons disappear? There are many theories. Climate change in the form of droughts or unseasonable cold are possibilities. Excessive hunting by American Indians is another possibility.

Undoubtedly remnant populations hung on longer in some isolated valleys. But the question is: for how long?

American Indian, Northern European, and Siberian folklore suggests that some may have survived up until just before the age of exploration. Peasants and tribal people may have done what came naturally when encountering rarities: kill them and eat them.

This story confirms the survival of this remnant population, but with a twist. Apparently Wisconsin's last pocket of survivors evolved into a smaller subspecies and at the end were all in captivity.

The source here is a world traveler who has some familiarity with the strange and exotic. Scott tells of his adventures in Borneo, the Amazon, and the Arctic as he holds court in the Richland Center VFW Bar (which for many years was the only place to get a beer in "dry" Richland Center).

🦢 🦢 🦢

I've seen a lot of strange things.

Two-headed snakes in Brazil. Albino monkeys in Thailand. An Eskimo boy brought up by polar bears. Even spent a night with Siamese-twin bar girls in Shanghai at the end of World War Two—a two-fer.

But one of the weirdest things I ever came across was right here in Richland County. Yup, dwarf mastodons out by Boaz in the Town of Dayton. Teeny-tiny little mastodons. A big bull was about the size of a miniature collie.

My great-uncle Boone said the settlers originally found them all along Mill Creek from Orion to Bosstown. There were some west to Five Points and Wild Rose. By the turn of the century they were pretty much confined to just south of Boaz and Fox Hollow.

They say they were big once, thousands of years ago. But the stuff they ate got scarce and the Kickapoo hunted the dickens out of them. Yup, gettin' small was just what they needed to do to survive. They didn't need as much food and they could hide in little cracks in the rocks.

The hollows and gullies were ideal for them. Out of the way and all. Also you have those sheltered south-facing spots where even in the worst winters there's a little green grass or other plants, especially if a spring bubbles up right there.

They started to die out during the Depression. I was a kid, of course, but I remember the grownups talking about it. There were big arguments about the die-off and what was causing it. Probably a lot of things. That stuff's never simple. At least that's what them environmentalists say.

A lot of the arguments were about accusations. Really bitter stuff. Some people said others were killing and eating the little critters. Could be times were pretty hard and sometimes people were pretty darn hungry. The old women did have recipes and the meat was said to taste good.

But as I said, there were other things going on too. A lot of those choice little spots where they lived got used up. Yup, good sites for cabins, hell, cattle sheds too. And the surrounding trees got logged off.

Great-uncle Boone had an idea that could be it too. He claimed that the population went down as the numbers of stray dogs and cats increased. It was about the time when farmers were letting dogs and cats find their own food.

A dog could kill even the biggest one. Cats carried off the babies. I even heard of a cat adopting some little ones instead of eating them.

Anyhow, by the late 1930s, they were pretty scarce. People started to catch the ones that were left. They turned them into pets. Sort of like how all these old ladies have these tiny little dogs now.

Problem was they didn't get no more babies. Yup, they just didn't breed when they were tamed. By the time I came back from the war, they had disappeared. I hear the Winkles had the last one and that it passed on in 1944.

There used to be something left over from them back in the fifties. Some in family pictures. Some little skulls used as ashtrays. But I haven't seen anything like that in years.

At one time I had a wallet made of their hide. The Old Lady had steak knives with their little ivory tusks for handles. A man up in Nevels Corners had a stuffed one.

I guess the lesson is that we gotta take care of stuff. And that we can't be sure how it all fits together. And how one thing leads to another. I guess anything we have—including ourselves—could end up that way. Dead. Wiped out. Extinct. Kaput. End of the line. Yup!

Lake Winnebago's Giant Sturgeon

W*isconsin's seldom-seen creatures fall mostly outside the bounds of established zoology. Weird beasts and biological oddities have definite storyteller appeal.*

Tales about widely known forms of wildlife usually fall into two other traditional story forms: the hunting story and the fishing story. Within these genres there is plenty of opportunity for embellishment and enlargement. The "big buck" hunting story and the "whopper" fishing story are familiar terrain to anyone who has visited a country tavern or bait shop.

Folklorists usually make a distinction between these hunting and fishing stories and a classic tall tale. The hunting and fishing stories focus on the activity rather than the object of pursuit; traditional tall tales cast their creatures in larger-than-human terms.

Occasionally one finds a hybrid story that draws upon both the sportsperson themes and the ominous monster archetype. Wisconsin has unusually large black bears said to be inhabited by spirits, coyotes as reincarnated rogues, and wily muskies evading the hook through supernatural means.

But there is another, rarer category of these elusive and mystical prey categories that harkens back to humanity's dimmest memories. There in the dark and primitive recesses of our subconscious lurk the prehistoric and primordial beasts that gave our ancestors nightmares.

Park the car on Harbor Road in Brothertown and follow a limping fellow out onto a frozen Lake Winnebago. Nathan tells a tale about the one that everyone hopes gets away.

💥 💥 💥

There's been a story of the Giant Sturgeon in Lake Winnebago ever since humans have fished this place.

Dad had a Brothertown Indian grandmother and she told him that the Winnebagos and Potawatomis talked about "the great one." You hear that type of thing from people in the old pioneer families.

This isn't the only place in Wisconsin that you hear such stories. Down on the Madison lakes and north of the Prairie du Sac dam on the Wisconsin River, you hear about other monster sturgeon. In fact, a huge sturgeon in Lake Mendota caused Loch Ness-type stories in the early part of this century.

Our Giant Sturgeon is at least thirty foot long. I've had it pass under my ice-fishing holes and it looks like a submarine. It's big enough that I could make out its shape through three feet of ice.

It links us to the past in a way no other living thing does. That's because it's either a remnant descendant of an ancient subspecies or it's actually a survivor from prehistoric times. The only reason it might be the latter is that sturgeons have the feel of things that are quite ancient and it would take a long time to grow to that size down in the cool depths.

There's always something about a big creature in the water that gives you that shrinking feeling between the legs. It goes back to stories of Job and to the Odyssey. The creatures of the water get in our minds like sea serpents or leviathan. After all, that thing described in the Book of Job in the Bible has to be one of the most horrifying descriptions ever written.

Why do we project these horrible images on large water beasts? I can't say for certain, but maybe it's an echo of a past we fear—even in ourselves. Maybe it's that connection to the primitive appetite, machine-like gnawing, and a brutal and insatiable instinct. The instinct that makes animals kill.

But maybe it's something else we fear. Maybe the presence of greater forces, godlike in some ways and yet demonic. Maybe we fear their judgment and retribution.

We've had disappearances on Lake Winnebago. Yet it's hard to believe that even a thirty-foot sturgeon could swallow a grown person. Maybe a child.

I'm pretty sure it got my buddy's yellow lab. Old Rex was fetching sticks offshore from Eckers Lakeland, south of Quinney. We were laughing at the dog's antics when all of a sudden he went down. It was like he was yanked down.

People have asked me for years where you can see the Giant Sturgeon. That's a hard question to answer. I've only seen it for sure five times in fifty years on the lake. Maybe a dozen other times when I thought it was there like with Old Rex.

I've heard of sightings all over Lake Winnebago, over by Menasha, across at Oshkosh, and down at Fond du Lac. It seems to be particularly fond of the Brothertown and High Cliff areas. But it's been seen even up in Lake Butte des Morts, Lake Poygan, and Partridge Lake.

There's a school of thought that says it's still breeding with the regular sturgeon and could create some more giants. They think some really big ones in the Wisconsin River may have come from spawning on the Fox River that got through the old Portage Canal. I don't know about that.

I do know that a friend of mine, who was fooling around with a fourteen-inch sucker for bait, latched onto something pretty dramatic. It jerked his heavy test line like a whip, pulled the boat on a twenty-foot jolt, and cracked the rod and took his line.

Another guy got a spear into it through the ice last winter. What a joke! What was he thinking about? It didn't even slow the bugger down. Just sucked the spear right down the hole and was gone.

But I don't encourage people to mess around with it. It's not a thing to laugh about. When I was a boy, I dove off a rowboat and it brushed right by me. You saw how I limp. Well, I consider myself lucky to be walking at all.

PART THREE

Lessons and Legacies— Teaching Through Stories

The Shining Boy

Almost all cultures have stories relating to the formation of con-stellations, stars, and other heavenly objects. In the Northern Hemi-sphere, the North Star draws considerable attention.

Many of the North American Indian tribes have tales revolving around the North Star. The subjects and storylines are diverse, but there is often a shared theme of setting an example. Exemplary actions and lives are frequently equated with our guiding star.

Such stories are usually simple and straightforward. They are meant to convince young people of the virtue of persistence and the value of their untapped potential. They are balm on the wounds of set-backs, defeats, and frustrations.

A Wausau health care worker named Sharon remembers a ver-sion told by her Potawatomi grandmother at a family gathering in Forest County.

🌿 🌿 🌿

Grandmother always started a story with the words, "a long, long time ago, before last week. . ."

She said she heard this story from her grandfather and that it explained the connection between the North Star and the first eclipse. She called the North Star "The Shining Boy."

I'll try to tell it as I remember it, but I worry that a bit of high school science class will creep in. On top of that, my Polish and German relatives may have turned it around in my mind.

A long, long time ago, before last week, the people always came to a summer festival. They came to dance and sing and eat. They always had a wonderful time at this festival.

But one year, the festival came and the opening ceremonies were disrupted. The Sun was blocked out by darkness. The Earth grew quiet and all the animals stood still.

A chill fell on the Earth. The festival stopped. People cried and ran in circles. The chiefs called a council.

The chiefs talked for a long time and asked the medicine men what to do. But the chiefs and the medicine men didn't know what to do.

So the warriors said they would do something. The biggest and strongest warrior said he would knock the cover off the Sun with his spear. He threw it as hard as he could and it went up, up, and almost to the Sun. But it turned around and fell through the darkness and killed the warrior.

A boy with shining eyes and a shining smile asked if he could try, but the other warriors pushed him away and told him he was too little.

They prepared a path for the warrior who was the best runner and jumper. That warrior took a big lead, ran, and jumped up to pull the cover off the Sun. But he didn't get high enough and he fell into a lake and drowned.

Again the Shining Boy asked to try. This time they roughly told him to go away. They told him he was being foolish.

Next, all the young warriors readied their tomahawks to throw at the cover on the Sun. They reached way back and threw as hard as they could. The tomahawks went high—but not high enough—and they fell through the shadows and split open the heads of those who threw them.

For the third time, the Shining Boy asked if he could try to uncover the Sun. This time, the people laughed and yelled insults and told the boy to keep quiet.

Now, the old women said they would make a fire. It was their plan to boil a big pot of water and steam the cover off the Sun. But the steam did not reach high enough and the pressure in the pot was too great. It blew up and scalded the old women.

Finally, the oldest chief said to the people: "Let the boy try, everything else has failed." The old chief put his hands on the boy's head in a blessing.

The Shining Boy said a prayer to the Creator. Then he ran swiftly up a path to the top of a hill. As he neared the top, he pulled back the light little arrow in his light little bow. He flung himself off the top rock of the hill and his little arrow caught the great wind.

The arrow went up, up, up. The Shining Boy did not aim at the center of the cover on the Sun. He aimed right at the edge. And his arrow went true. The arrow nicked the edge of the cover and the great wind grabbed the edge and tore back the cover.

And that is how the Sun was freed in what was called "the year the Sun was trapped in the lodge."

What became of the Shining Boy? They could not find him at the base of the rock at the top of the hill. But that night there was a new star in the northern sky. The medicine men said it was the Shining By. And from that time forward, he guided the people on all the paths laid out by the Creator.

Black River's Gloomnadoom

Local mythical creatures usually fall within the realms of whimsy or horror. Wisconsin folklore seldom produces fanciful beings that represent the more subtle traits of pathos, sadness, and regret. Even the "teaching" stories avoid despondent themes.

Folktales rarely celebrate negative subjects unless there is an outrageous component that piques our fancy or a lesson that resonates in our hearts. In the days before psychotherapists, the village storytellers performed the counseling function for those in a funk or experiencing the blues.

Much of that old-time knowledge has been lost among European Americans. Among American Indians, it is frequently connected to spiritual traditions and thus inappropriate for inclusion under the irreverent heading of "tall tales."

My travels have introduced me to many wistful tales that brim over with feelings of loss and yearning. This is the only one I found that went deeper into the terrain of misery—and hints at laughter in the process.

The story setting is a front porch in the Jackson County village of Melrose. Sidney, a retired technical college instructor, remembers a childhood tale.

🔥 🔥 🔥

The Gloomnadoom roams from Hatfield to Brice Prairie.

Our scattered Scottish family has known of the Gloomnadoom for a hundred years. They may have brought it with them from Scotland and then to Vernon and Monroe counties. It is hard to tell since recorded Scottish lore makes no reference to the Gloomnadoom.

The Gloomnadoom is a strange little thing. It is hard to describe. It is smallish, maybe eighteen to twenty-four inches high. Wears a black, hooded, ankle-length robe—like a monk.

You never see a face—just a darkness in the hood. No hands either—just big draping sleeves. There's a hint of feet—some kind of pointy shoes.

The funny thing about the Gloomnadoom is that the person afflicted by it almost never sees it. Oh, they might see it stalking them initially. But by the time it's really got a grip on someone, they have no idea what is going on.

I had an uncle who had a terminal Gloomnadoom. First, it kind of perched on his shoulder. Gave him a crick in the neck that the chiropractor could not get out. It definitely affected his mood. He was down in the dumps something terrible.

Then it got heavier, denser. It does not get bigger. It starts out with the density of granite and ends up like lead. You can imagine that a day of that on your neck and a night of it sleeping on your chest would wear you down.

Finally, it turns mean at the end. With my uncle, it just started riding on his back like he was a horse. He got fidgety and hyper. It dug its spurs into his ribs and whipped his rear end with a riding crop. It beat him and beat him and worked him over good until he just laid down and died.

The Gloomnadoom can do its dirty work in a variety of ways. Heart attacks are a big item. Strokes too. But I have heard of everything from ulcers to total insanity. It afflicts many people along the Black River. Yet you will never see it mentioned in a medical file or autopsy report.

The chief symptoms of the Gloomnadoom are the dees and disses. Things like dejected, depressed, defeated, deserted, deprived, and deluded. Things like discouraged, dispirited, dessicated, destitute, desperate, despondent, and despairing.

Because the Gloomnadoom kind of creeps up on you, the only antidote is friendship. You need a friend or a buddy who can yell "duck" when it leaps for your neck. You need a pal who will pry the sucker off your back. You need someone who will take a baseball bat to that little robed blankety-blank and beat it and you until it lets go. That's friendship!

It is said that you will never suffer from the Gloomnadoom if you take preventive steps. A friend can help you fight it. But it takes more subtle steps to ward it off entirely.

It is said that those who surround themselves with children's laughter are totally immune. It is said that those who experience their

144

spiritual faith in a way that electrifies their physical being repel the Gloomnadoom. It is said that a good marriage to a spunky and earthy woman provides pretty good resistance too.

The other so-called cures are a mixed bag. Take beer and brandy for example. I know some regular drinkers who never have the Gloomnadoom's shadow fall on them. For others, the Gloomnadoom can sneak right out of the bottle and get heavier with each drink.

It works that way with taverns too. In some places, the good feelings run so thick that the Gloomnadoom can't get in the door. In other places, it's practically tending bar—pouring doubles and playing those crying songs on the jukebox.

Same with churches. I have known places that are lit up with smiles as warm as a potbelly stove full of cured white oak. I have seen some others so full of fear and constipation that they looked like a lemon suckers' convention.

So in the end, the best thing you can do is hang out with the right people in the right places. It is like my eight-year-old grandson says: "Happiness is a choice." But it sure seems like it is hard for some people to make that obvious choice.

So I think we are lucky to have this Gloomnadoom. Yes, you heard me. It keeps us on our toes and keeps our priorities straight.

People in other places may just have a sourpuss or two in the zoning office or on the chamber of commerce or with the church committee. Not really enough to keep you on the right track. Not at all like having a Gloomnadoom to warn us away from those bad moods.

St. Croix River's Little People

Cross-fertilization of folktales is a relatively common phenomenon. However, it usually takes the form of subtle expropriation of a character type or storyteller. When this borrowing occurs between ethnic groups and races, it is common for the borrowers to be in complete denial about the origin of the story.

There is little in the way of open story-grafting between distinct groups. Such folklore transfers are only admitted between members

145

of larger extended families. Thus, the storytellers' unspoken code permits Ottawa to Ojibwe, Russian to Ukrainian, and Swiss to German borrowing.

Mobility and intermarriage serve to create some unique stories in the modern global village. One can find a family blending Norwegian and Hmong traditions in the Chippewa Valley. In Milwaukee, another clan whips up a new tradition from their German and Tibetan components. Along the lower Wisconsin River, a war-weary Vietnam veteran and a Salvadoran survivor teach their children a vision of peace.

Honesty compels an admission that considerable ambivalence exists toward the circumstances and relationships that generate these mixtures. Society is not nearly as accepting of refugees as our national myth would have us believe. War brides and other foreign spouses do not always find the welcome mat out in the in-laws' hometown.

Such circumstances have a way of mellowing over time. Today's immigrants are tomorrow's old families. Long intervals of intergroup exchange can make for interesting story stews. The story below is the most self-conscious and overt mixture I could find.

Mary Helene, a thirty-something red-haired waitress in St. Croix Falls, knows this tale from repeated family telling. Stop in her cafe and wait for the breakfast rush to end.

🌿 🌿 🌿

The Little People are the special beings of the St. Croix River.

They are special in many ways. Special because they are magical and act out of good intentions. And special because they came about through a melange of traditions.

In my Irish family—with bits of French and Chippewa thrown in—it is said that the Little People along the river resulted from the combination of Chippewa little beings, Irish leprechauns, German elves, and European wood sprites.

But we know the Irish element is still strong. The Little People—men and women—still smoke the clay pipes, and their hats and bonnets still have the look of County Cork.

146

Now, for most people, this is a touching story of the virtues of cooperation and good that come from the mingling of peoples and traditions. For a few thickheads, it is proof of the perversions of miscegenation.

The Little People are the guardians of the St. Croix River. The old Ojibwe little beings had a long tradition of calming the lakes and rivers. They still do that up in the Boundary Waters. But in this area they intermarried with leprechauns and such and acquired more skills.

My pagan women friends tell me that the cross-breeding of different supernatural beings usually makes for a bad combination. They say if you cross a North American Manitou with a German poltergeist or a Scottish bodach you end up with a psycho-spirit on drugs. The leprechaun and Little Beings cross went the opposite direction. Almost like angels, or a least cherubs.

The resulting Little People are an odd assortment of women with freckled high cheekbones and auburn braids and dark-haired men with blue eyes. They can be found from Osceola up to Danbury.

It is said that the Little People are visible only to children. I saw them as a child. But I could swear I've glimpsed them since then. As children, we had a way to communicate with them that involved whispering into cracks in rocks where springs gurgled out. Then we listened to the bubbling and dripping to hear the reply.

It was said that if you whispered the name of someone polluting the water into the spring crack, that the Little People would take action. They would muddy that person's well water and make their tap water run filthy. Their bathroom shower would spray sewage and their toilet ran with blood. Not to mention the vomiting and the runs that they gave a polluter.

The messages in those bubbling springs are said to be many. The Little People are fine teachers. They talk mostly of living in harmony with the Earth. How to care for the waters. How to care for the plants and animals. And how different people can live in harmony with each other.

All the lessons of all time are in that bubbling water. Listen and the Little People will tell how all life came out of water and how everything is washed down the rivers and into the sea in the end. They know all the secrets of the creeks, lakes, and oceans. They know the secrets of sharing water and blood.

The Good King

Male role models in folklore are often a mixed bag of muscle-bound, humorous, and hapless archetypes. Sometimes even the heroes lack depth and maturity.

The erosion of community, loosening of church connections, and deep disagreements about appropriate male behavior and values all contribute to the confusion about any male "ideal." The chasm between the strict (and often vengeful) patriarch and the fuzzy (and often ineffectual) "new age" male is wide and deep.

Folklore prescriptions and proscriptions about behavior are fairly common. Sadly, they are often on the level of "Thou shall not" commandments and offer little advice about personal growth and responsibility.

Within ethnic lore we see some hints of Old World concepts of the "good man." There, the roles of spouse, parent, and citizen find some definition. The parameters are usually drawn from the Judeo-Christian tradition, but echoes of earlier pagan times can sometimes be detected.

Here we have a rare type of story that focuses totally on male responsibility. It is all the more important for its placement in relatively unknown Belgian American traditions. The format is that of the ultimate patriarch: a king. Yet, the message is hardly one of royal privilege.

A referral sent me to Curran in southwestern Kewaunee County. Baking smells wafted out of Juliette's somewhat hidden cottage on Black Creek.

🌱 🌱 🌱

It took me many years to figure out the meaning of the story of the Good King.

148

When my great-aunt Marie told it to us as children we just thought of it as entertainment. We didn't realize that she was speaking to the boys about what sort of men to be. We didn't realize that she was speaking to the girls about what sort of sons to raise and what sort of men to wed.

Marie was one of those strong Belgian women who believed that the hand that rocks the cradle rules the world. She also was one to bring down wrath on wife beaters and on fathers whose children went hungry while the paycheck or crop proceeds disappeared in the tavern.

She understood that in her day, women often had limited options. As a result, she thought it was important for women to be cautious on the selection of mates. At the same time, she thought that women had a duty to raise decent men. She also thought that a standard of genuine manliness came from the old values.

As my great-aunt told the story, there was once a time of good kings, good lords, knights, and chieftains. It was a time when women could be chiefs too.

One day, strangers from a troubled land came to the Country of the Good King. In their suffering homeland they knew of war, hunger, and sick children. In the Country of the Good King they saw fat cattle, laughing children, and rosy-cheeked wives.

So they sought out the Good King. They had many questions to ask him about the blessings of his country. They followed the directions to the king's house. They were surprised that no army guarded the way.

When they reached the end of the road they were shocked to find no castle, no palace, and no fortress. Instead, there was a large farmhouse set in the middle of grain fields and pastures. A big jolly man came out to greet the strangers. When they asked to see the king, the big man laughed and informed them that they were looking at the king.

The Good King invited them in to dinner. They were seated at his side at a large table. Instead of princes and knights, the king dined with his children, grandchildren, and farmhands. Instead of royal musicians and jesters, the strangers heard laughter and cooing babies. The king toasted his wife and called blessings upon her.

The visitors thought that there must be a tricky side to this rustic king. Surely a ruler of such a rich land must possess hidden powers. Finally, they asked the Good King about the secret to his success.

He laughed and swept his hand wide. "Everything you need to know is in this room and on this farm," he said. He told them that a good kingdom is a warm family and a well-run farm.

149

The strangers were impressed by this wisdom and complimented the king on the quality of his advisers. Again the king laughed. He told them that in his kingdom the grandmothers pick the king and guide his actions. And he told them all the rules he observed as king.

When the strangers returned to their own land, they told the story of the Good King. The Good King surrounds himself with love. The Good King lives a life like those of the people.

He is a steward of his kingdom. He is guided by the thought of his grandchildren's grandchildren. He loves the land. He avoids the counsel of generals and listens to the women, from the youngest first-time mother to the oldest great-great-grandmother. A good king knows that the future is in the hands of those who care for the children.

The Good King believes that a land where children go hungry is a land without moral conviction. The Good King believes that a land where children are subjected to violence is a land run by villains. The Good King believes that land where women are abused is a land without a soul.

The travelers told their people all these things about the Land of the Good King. But the princes, lords, and regents of that suffering land had the travelers thrown in a dungeon to hide this knowledge. Nevertheless, the story of the Good King did survive and it gave the people of the suffering land hope. And the old women told the boys this story and they became better men.

Kickapoo Rose

American Indian references are common in Wisconsin folklore. All the present-day Wisconsin tribes find expression in tales connected to outdoor lore. In addition, pioneer era stories are filled with references to tribes no longer present in Wisconsin.

The tribal names Ottawa, Mascouten, Huron, Fox, and Sac are reference points for the mystery and romance of the frontier era. They fill our speech, maps, and legends with echoes of bygone days.

Perhaps no other displaced Wisconsin tribe has left a greater legacy than the Kickapoo. One can find references to Kickapoo hunters, scouts, and medicine men in stories from Green Bay to Hazel Green. Southwest Wisconsin is a particularly fertile territory for such tales.

As common as American Indian figures and Kickapoo references are in Wisconsin's European American legends, they are generally male characters. Our stories have often reduced American Indian women to sullen stereotypes and have labeled them with the pejorative term squaw.

Wisconsin tribes themselves were not egalitarian in terms of gender roles. As a general rule, hunting-based cultures elevated male status. Introduction of the fur trade by the British and French (and subsequent trade wars) heightened the male dominance. Women "leaders" were found only in cultures with settled agricultural villages.

So it should not be a surprise that Kickapoo women left such a faint imprint on the stories that survived down to today. My sources could steer me to only one such reference. Happily, it is as rich a reference as one could expect to find of a people whose wanderings and hardships are almost forgotten.

It is a tale rescued from extinction by a thoughtful young woman who spent many rewarding hours listening to the remembrances of older Kickapoo Valley residents. The setting is a warm corner of the old Kickapoo Exchange co-op on a cold winter's day.

Find out from Beth how a folktale tradition is told by women across gaps of culture and time.

🌿 🌿 🌿

This isn't really "my" story.

I wasn't born in the area. But it feels such a part of me. I can't imagine living anywhere else. That's why I love to listen to the old people.

Especially the women. There is so much wisdom and practical knowledge among those women. So much that comes down from many generations ago. Women tell stories differently.

Elsie first told me about Kickapoo Rose. She told many other local tales before she got around to Kickapoo Rose. She told stories in a long luxurious style that was like an afternoon in a bubble bath. She gave me a wonderful summer of stories before she died last winter.

But some of what I can tell you didn't come directly from Elsie. I had to draw some conclusions abut the meaning of the stories and their significance. I believe Elsie wanted me to think those things through. Especially with the Kickapoo Rose story.

Kickapoo Rose was many things. She was a teacher, a healer, an outdoorswoman, and maybe a sorceress. And she was called many names. Kickapoo Rose was just a label tacked on after she moved away.

Earlier she was called Coyote Woman, Woman of the River, Bone Woman, and Woman of the Cave. Kickapoo Rose apparently called herself these things in connection with stories she told to pioneer women and children.

Each story had a lesson to it, I guess. I have a feeling that there were lots more stories. Maybe if we listen closely to the other old women around here we'll find fragments of more stories.

This line of thinking is a lot different from the way the men told Kickapoo Rose stories. With them, it was always something about her being a good shot with a rifle, a good tracker of game, and a skilled survivalist. There were even stories about how she could outrun men and disarm knife-wielding hoodlums.

It was said that she ran from her home area near La Farge down to Prairie du Chien to bring help when madness struck a pioneer family. If you've driven Highway 27, you know that's not an easy jog.

Elsie said the men had other tales too. Things like Kickapoo Rose wrestling a bear. Or taming a mountain lion for a pet.

But I think there's more significance in the spiritual stories the women told. Like the one about Coyote Woman. Coyote Woman is the free spirit that lives in balance with nature. She is the woman who knows how to be close to the Earth and how to experience the joy of running in the woods.

Coyote Woman was seen running in the moonlight. She was even heard howling in exuberance. She was telling us to keep at least some space for that wildness in us. She was telling us that we must bear some responsibility for our wellness and freedom.

The Woman of the River was a different side of Kickapoo Rose. She was heavily identified with the Kickapoo River. Kind of a patron saint, if you will. A symbol of purity and renewal.

Woman of the River taught lessons that today we would call deep ecology. The river was the cycle of life. It was the symbol of the journey through life. And for women, it was also the river of life that flows through us. The lesson here was that women are the guardians of water and water itself is sacred.

Bone Woman was another link to the great cycle of life, only she focused on death. Kickapoo Rose was the pioneer equivalent of a grief counselor.

She understood death well. She knew when to cheat it and when to accept it. She knew the old herbal medicine that eased death for the dying, calmed the grieving. She performed an important function for isolated pioneer women.

Woman of the Cave was the most mysterious side of her. In a way, that was the dark side of Kickapoo Rose. But not an evil side. No, more of the deep soulful side of her that knew and accepted the bad things about humans.

She taught women how to draw strength out of bad experiences. But also how to find that cave within them. That deep fortress of protection, secret knowledge and faith. Woman of the Cave fit perfectly into our local landscape of hollows, caverns, and overhangs. It offered both a protection of the soul and a protection of the body that comes with sheltering places.

Kickapoo Rose is a different sort of story than other heroes you hear about. With the heroes, there are great things that we regular people can't hope to do. But with Kickapoo Rose, the whole point is that these things are within us all.

Here you have a young Indian woman on her own. She's probably a mixed blood Kickapoo with a bit of Winnebago and French in her background. Her tribe moves away. She is left in an uncertain status with an area that is just being taken over by newcomers.

What an intense experience that must have been. To learn to live outside of old structures, to learn to deal with alien people and to grow through all that.

I like to think that within each young girl there is a Kickapoo Rose. Deep inside there is a medicine woman and a woodswoman. Deep inside there is the inner strength to heal ourselves with our stories.

153

How Things Came to Be

American Indian oral traditions shape Wisconsin stories in countless ways. Our love of the land and our sense of spiritual awe at nature's wonders draw heavily upon the teachings of the first inhabitants.

This collection offers numerous stories with American Indian roots. Yet, I would never claim to have collected American Indian folklore. Among Wisconsin tribes, the oral traditions are inextricably linked to tribal history and spiritual practices. Such traditions should not fall victim to lazy categorization as "folktales."

Those who wish to explore these story traditions can find a number of works by academics and spiritual teachers that can introduce the outsider to this hidden world. Readers of such works will be immediately struck with the number of themes and archetypes shared among all cultures.

One sturdy area of oral tradition that is shared worldwide is the Creation story. All peoples used stories to explain the origin of the physical world and the things in it. These stories range from holy writ to hilarious to hoary to humble.

The ones below are offered as exhibits of the nonreligious variations. They are lighthearted responses to children's inevitable questions of "why."

The source, Naomi, is Potawatomi-Menominee-Dutch. But she offers the stories up as things grandmothers say in Forest County, not as enshrined parts of any tribal or ethnic traditions. Join her for a glass of fresh-squeezed berry juice in her Laona bungalow.

🌿 🌿 🌿

The old ones always had answers for the little ones.

Children always ask playful questions at that tender age that calls for playful answers. How do you use just facts to answer a questions about why there are bears or why does it snow?

The child who asks such things usually wants a story, not an answer. When they're four or five, a textbook answer would go right over their heads anyway.

When they ask where things come from, they're partly trying to figure out an order for things. But they're also testing you, trying to see how you respond.

Busy parents often fail these tests. But grandparents have it down to a fine art. They polish these things and hand down the good ones to the next generation.

My grandmother gave me the berry story. As a little girl, I asked her where berries came from. She pointed to the stars.

She said that in the time of giants, the berries grew in the sky and the giants picked them up there. But later, when the people came to Earth, they wanted some berries down here. An old grandmother shook her stick at the stars and told the berries to come down.

Sure enough, the stars listened. They turned into shooting stars. And over the years, enough shooting stars came down to start berry patches all over. Grandmother said that a really good meteor shower guaranteed a good berry crop the next year.

Aunt Lucy told me about the bears. Children are fascinated by bears. They wonder if we're related to bears the way we're related to apes. She told us it's the other way around.

Bears, she said, came from people. More particularly, they came from lazy men. Aunt Lucy said there were some men who just had to sleep the winter away.

These lazy men didn't do a thing to help their families in the winter. They didn't hunt or fish to feed the children and the old ones. They didn't get firewood or furs to keep warm. They just wanted to sleep.

Finally, their wives got tired of that. Tired of their snoring and sighing. So they carried them out into the woods and stuck them in holes in the ground and hollow trees.

And a funny thing happened over the winter. The lazy men grew fur and they grew claws. When they came out of the holes in the spring, they were bears.

A few lazy women went off to join them, thinking that this sleeping all winter is a good deal. But they all paid the price for this foolishness because a bear has to search for food all summer long and get fat.

Dad said that his grandmother told him about the wild rice. There are lots of stories about the wild rice and how it was a gift

155

from the Creator or how people had to wander in the wilderness to find it.

But Dad's story was more about how the rice got into the lakes. He was told that having the rice is payment for living in a harsh place. It's our reward for sticking it out through the winter.

There was a time when there was a really long, hard winter. A winter that started in early October and was still hanging on in late April. May came and there was still ice on the lakes.

The ice finally melted and it was time to fish, so the people all got in their boats. They went out on a nice day but a storm came up. They were driven off the lake by hard, freezing rain. The freezing rain was like seeds of grain.

But the people noticed that in the following summer, there was a new plant growing on the lake. And they discovered that it was a good food that could be kept through the winter.

So they found that every time there was a hard winter that lingered way into spring and kept them from fishing a lake, there was wild rice growing in that lake to make up for it. So you knew that freezing rain is good for something.

Old Granddad over by Crandon had the funniest story about trout. He told it with such style and enthusiasm. Sometimes he would even hop up on the furniture.

Trout, he said, didn't start out as fish. He said they tasted so much better than other fish for a reason. Then he would jump up and flap his arms and say that trout were really partridges.

Now you have to understand that his mother was talked about as a great cook. Her top specialties were partridge and trout. She made her dishes so tasty that you couldn't tell partridge from trout.

She told everybody that trout were just partridges that decided to live in the water. I guess they were jealous of the fish. While the partridge had to hide in spruce trees to keep warm and hunt for seeds, the fish were down in that water eating minnows and crawfish. No below zero temperatures and howling winds down there.

At this point, Granddad wold make like he had flown down out of the sky and dived into the water. He'd make swimming motions. Mostly like he was doing a breast stroke.

So eventually, some partridges decided to move into the water. The other fish said, okay, but you have to give up your feathers and your wings. The partridges said, okay, but we want to be different from fish in some way. The other fish said, okay, you can taste different.

156

Then Granddad would round his mouth like a fish and bend his arms in and move them like fins. And he'd chase us around and say we looked like tasty crawfish.

Bathtub Mary had a good one too. She was old, a little crazy, and she slept in an old bathtub. But she knew lots of the grand-mother stories.

The one she told me when I was a little girl was about the fir trees. I always liked fir trees, they're the prettiest members of the evergreen family. They're so delicate and they dance in the wind.

When I was a little girl I asked Bathtub Mary why the fir trees were different. She told me it was the old problem of wanting to be something different from what we are.

She said the firs were fern plants long ago. But they were jealous of the tall, swaying pine trees. And they whined just like children, crying to be trees.

Finally, the wind granted their wish. They became fir trees. They soon learned that it was not easy to be trees. The storms strained the branches. The heavy snows cracked the limbs. Lightning struck the trunks. The whole thing was a lesson in what happens wishing to be something big.

There are many stories like that. One old lady up at Keshena told me that all the old Wisconsin stories have a lesson in them. She said the stories are little messages left for us by the generations of the past. We just have to listen close to figure out what they mean.